IVO DRPIC

# Sketching and Rendering Interior Spaces

## IVO D. DRPIC

WHITNEY LIBRARY OF DESIGN
An imprint of Watson-Guptill Publications/New York

This book is dedicated to my lovely wife, Consuelito,
for her help, constant support, and encouragement

First published in New York by Whitney Library of Design
an imprint of Watson-Guptill Publications
a division of Billboard Publications, Inc.
1515 Broadway, New York, NY 10036

**Library of Congress Cataloging-in-Publication Data**
Drpic, Ivo D.
  Sketching and rendering interior spaces : practical
techniques for professional results / Ivo Drpic.
    p.  cm.
  Includes index.
  ISBN 0-8230-4854-3
  ISBN 0-8230-4853-5 (pk.)
1. Architectural rendering—Techniques.  2. Interior
architecture— Designs and plans.  3. Dry marker drawing—
Technique.  4. Visual perception—Technique.  I. Title.
NA2780.D77 1988                     88-5469
720′.28′4—dc 19                        CIP

Distributed in the United Kingdom by Phaidon Press Ltd.
Littlegate House, St. Ebbe's St., Oxford

Copyright © 1988 by Ivo D. Drpic

Manufactured in Japan

First printing, 1988

1  2  3  4  5  6  7  8  9/93  92  91  90  89  88

**Front matter illustrations:**

Half-title page:
  Preliminary Study of a Residential Media Room
  Architect: Ivo D. Drpic and Associates

Title page:
  Preliminary Study for a Hotel Lobby
  Architect: Ivo D. Drpic and Associates

Acknowledgments page:
  Preliminary Study of Offices for Houtronics, Houston, Texas
  Architect: Ivo D. Drpic and Associates

All drawings in this book are by Ivo D. Drpic
unless otherwise noted.

Senior Editor: Julia Moore
Designer: Bob Fillie
Production Manager: Hector Campbell

# Contents

THANKS

to my parents, Susy Drpic and the late Antonio Drpic,
for their support and encouragement;

to my daughters, Jeancarla, Giovanna, and Geraldine,
for their help on this book;

to my grandparents, Rachel and Eric Eisenstaedt,
and also Sigrid E. Rosenthal, all of whom contributed
to my education;

to Julia Moore at Whitney Library of Design
for her advice and suggestions, without which
this would be a lesser book.

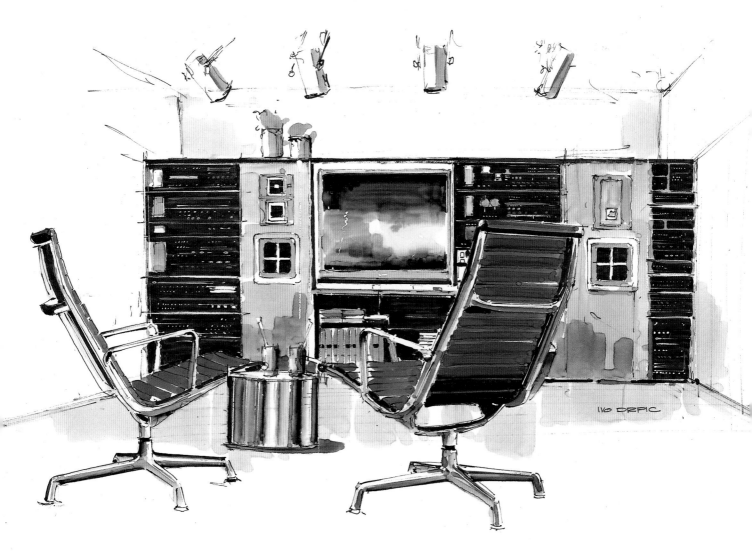

# Preface

This book has been created with one purpose in mind: to teach the art of sketching interior architecture quickly, accurately, and effectively. Architects and interior designers are very busy people who have to communicate concepts and ideas at every stage of the design process. They need to be able to produce images throughout the continuum, from the first glimmerings of a design idea through the advertising and promotion of a successful project.

Sketches answer every need for interiors work. The very process of sketching encourages new design ideas. Sketches are quick to execute and are enormously responsive to depicting the look and feel of surfaces and finishes. And sketching can also persuasively convey the mood or spirit of a space.

Good sketching skills are, in fact, a practical business asset. They eliminate the need to pay a professional renderer and shorten the costly time between the germination of a design concept and its acceptance as a paying project.

This book is a complete pictorial course in sketching interior spaces, beginning with a review of how different kinds of sketches are used at the various stages of the design process. In highly visual terms, it shows how to organize space with perspectives and plans and it demonstrates, step by step, how to progress from a blank sheet of sketch paper to a presentation-quality rendering.

# The Basics of Sketching

## USES, TECHNIQUES, MATERIALS, AND PERSPECTIVES

**Preliminary Study for Sugarland Mall, Sugarland, Texas**
Architect: Ivo D. Drpic and Associates, Houston, Texas

From rough doodles to polished renderings, architectural sketches are the designer's most responsive and most persuasive tool. This section shows the many uses of sketches, offers techniques for freeing the hand, suggests simple materials and equipment, and presents simplified techniques for organizing interior spaces with perspectives, views, and plans.

IVO DRPIC/87

# THE USES OF SKETCHES

SKETCHES ARE USED BY DESIGN PROFESSIONALS TO VISUALIZE DESIGN IDEAS — PRIMARILY FOR OTHERS, BUT ALSO FOR THEMSELVES. SKETCHES ARE A VERY BASIC TOOL FOR COMMUNICATING YOUR PLANS FOR A MASS OR SPACE. AND ALTHOUGH SKETCHING IS A BASIC AND ABSOLUTELY NECESSARY SKILL TO HAVE, IT DEMANDS MENTAL AND PHYSICAL DISCIPLINE TO DO IT WELL. IT ALSO REQUIRES PRACTICE.

WHAT IS A SKETCH? IT IS A QUICKLY MADE, DIRECT, AND UNLABORED DRAWING. THERE IS A DIFFERENCE BETWEEN SKETCHING AS DONE BY A DESIGN PROFESSIONAL AND A LAYPERSON: ARCHITECTURAL SKETCHES MUST INCORPORATE PROPORTION AND SCALE.

ARCHITECTURAL SKETCHES RANGE FROM QUICK, PERSONAL VISUAL NOTES TO PRESENTATION RENDERING- QUALITY DRAWINGS. SKETCHES INCREASE IN COMPLEXITY AND COMPLETENESS AS A PROJECT PROGRESSES FROM THE EARLIEST IDEAS STAGES THROUGH THE DEVELOPMENT AND AND APPROVAL PHASES. THUS THERE ARE PERSONAL SKETCHES, CONCEPT SKETCHES, DESIGN DEVELOPMENT AND PRESENTATION SKETCHES, AND PRESENTATION RENDERINGS.

ALL SKETCHES ARE ESSENTIALLY LINE DRAWINGS, BUT ALMOST ANY SKETCH MAY BE ENHANCED BY THE USE OF COLOR.

GERALDINE DRPIC

# TAKING AND MAKING NOTES

SKETCHES MADE FOR PERSONAL USE RANGE FROM
JOTTINGS OF A DESIGN IDEA OR "INSPIRATION"

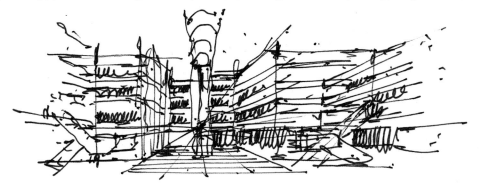

TO VISUAL NOTES MADE IN THE FIELD

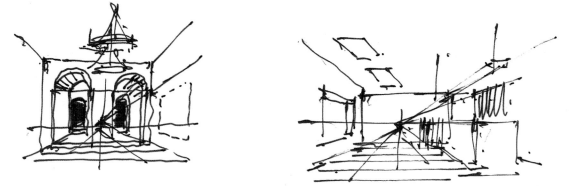

TO A ROUGH SKETCH TO SHARE, PERHAPS, WITH A
COLLEAGUE.

IN INTERIORS WORK, SKETCHES ARE PARTICULARLY VALUABLE BECAUSE THEY ARE IDEAL FOR CONVEYING THE SUBTLETIES OF TEXTURE AND FINISHES OF SURFACES. SKETCHES AND RENDERINGS MADE ON A CADD SYSTEM, FOR EXAMPLE, CANNOT BEGIN TO APPROACH THE RICHNESS OF A COLOR SKETCH.

TWO OF THE MOST IMPORTANT ELEMENTS TO KEEP IN MIND WHEN YOU ARE EXECUTING A SKETCH ARE <u>PROPORTION</u> AND <u>SCALE</u>.

FOR EXAMPLE, LET'S SEE WHAT HAPPENS TO A SKETCH OF AN INTERIOR SPACE WHEN THE HEIGHT OF A PERSON IS CHANGED.

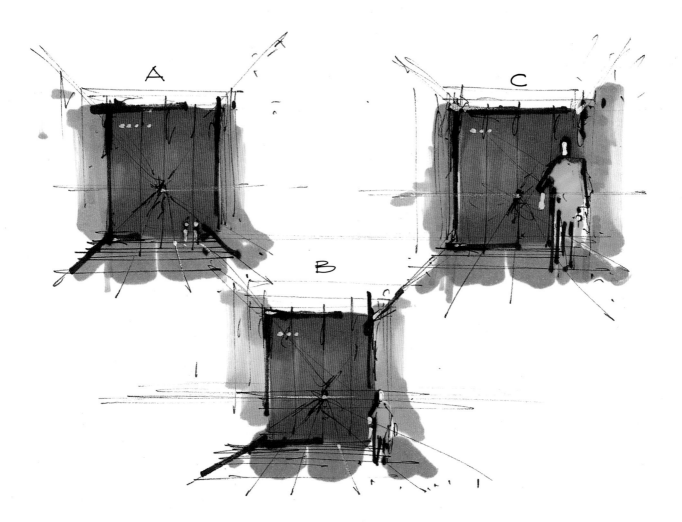

IN SKETCH A, THE SPACE LOOKS MONUMENTAL. HOWEVER, IN SKETCH B, CHANGING THE HEIGHT OF THE PERSON MAKES THE SPACE FIT MORE TO SCALE. IF YOU KEEP ENLARGING THE SIZE OF THE PERSON, AS IN SKETCH C, YOU WILL NOTICE THAT THIS SPACE IS NOT VERY LARGE.

SO WHEN YOU ARE SKETCHING EITHER A NEW DESIGN OR JUST TAKING NOTES, ALWAYS KEEP IN MIND A SENSE OF PROPORTION AND SCALE.

## SKETCHING EXISTING SPACES

AT FIRST, CAREFULLY OBSERVE THE SPACE IN ORDER TO ANALYZE OR FAMILIARIZE YOURSELF WITH IT. OBSERVE DETAILS OR SOME OTHER IMPORTANT ELEMENTS. RELATE THE HEIGHT OF THE PERSONS TO THE HEIGHT OF THE SPACE BY SELECTING SOME KEY ELEMENT. FOR INSTANCE, TAKE THE DIMENSION OF A TILE OR AN EXISTING GRID, AND FIND OUT HOW MANY TIMES IT IS REPEATED.

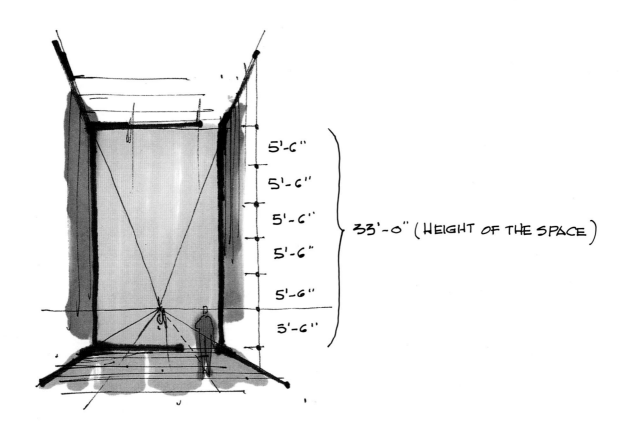

5'-6"
5'-6"
5'-6"
5'-6"
5'-6"
5'-6"

} 33'-0" (HEIGHT OF THE SPACE)

## CONCEPT SKETCHES

AS THE NAME SUGGESTS, THESE ARE VERY SIMPLE
DRAWINGS WHICH CONTAIN FEW PEN STROKES AND,
IN SOME CASES, A TOUCH OF COLOR. THESE FEW
LINES REFLECT THE ESSENCE OF AN IDEA.

# DESIGN DEVELOPMENT SKETCHES

DURING THE PROCESS OF DESIGNING AN INTERIOR SPACE, IT IS NECESSARY TO CARRY OR DEVELOP THE ORIGINAL IDEAS (CONCEPTS) INTO A MORE REALISTIC APPROACH THAT WILL DEMONSTRATE HOW THE CONCEPT WORKS. FOR INSTANCE, THESE SKETCHES SHOW IN MORE DETAIL SOME ELEMENTS OF THE DESIGN. THESE KINDS OF DESIGN DEVELOPMENT SKETCHES ARE VERY USEFUL FOR STUDYNG DETAILS, COMMUNICATING WITH THE REST OF THE TEAM, AND FOR POLISHING THE DESIGN.

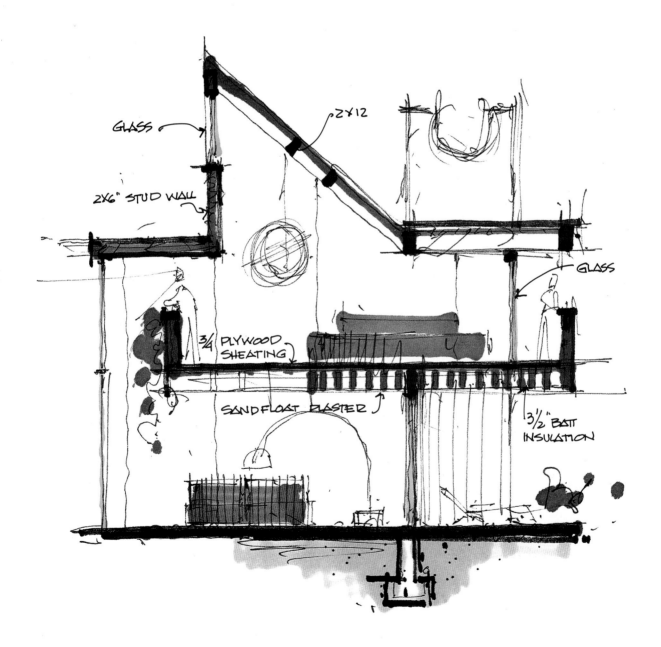

IN ORDER TO EXPRESS YOUR IDEAS, NO MATTER HOW SIMPLE THEY MAY BE, YOU SHOULD TAKE A PEN AND PAPER AND START REGISTERING (SKETCHING) YOUR THOUGHTS.

MAKE SMALL SKETCHES THAT ARE NO LARGER THAN 2"×2" OR 3"×3". THEN LOOSEN UP YOUR HAND BY DOODLING UNTIL THE RIGHT IDEA OR CONCEPT COMES UP. TRY TO PRACTICE MAKING SMALL SKETCHES AS MUCH AS POSSIBLE. DO NOT WORRY IF AT FIRST YOUR SKETCHES LOOK VERY STIFF. WITH PRACTICE YOU WILL IMPROVE AND GAIN CONFIDENCE.

## PRESENTATION SKETCHES

THESE SKETCHES ARE A LITTLE MORE INFORMATIVE THAN CONCEPT SKETCHES. THEY ARE USUALLY DONE IN HOUSE. YET, THEY ARE NOT AS ABSTRACT AS THE CONCEPT SKETCHES. THEY USE PERSPECTIVE, COLOR, AND OTHER ARCHITECTURAL DETAILS, SUCH AS TEXTURE, PATTERN, AND MATERIALS, IN ORDER TO CONVEY THE MESSAGE OR IDEA TO THE CLIENT.

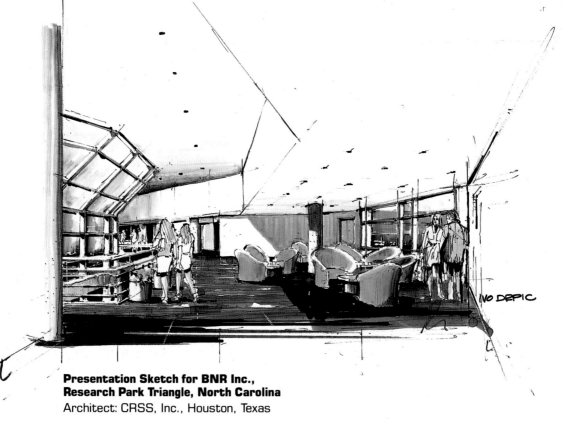

**Presentation Sketch for BNR Inc.,**
**Research Park Triangle, North Carolina**
Architect: CRSS, Inc., Houston, Texas

# PRESENTATION RENDERINGS

THESE KINDS OF DRAWINGS ARE MORE FINISHED, AND, IN MOST CASES, THEY ARE DONE BY OUTSIDE PROFESSIONAL DELINEATORS. THEY ARE OFTEN VERY RIGID IN APPEARANCE. GENERALLY, THESE KINDS OF FINAL DRAWINGS ARE USED FOR BROCHURES AND MEETINGS. THEY ARE ALSO SEEN BY PEOPLE FROM ALL WALKS OF LIFE WHO DO NOT UNDERSTAND SKETCHES OR BLUE PRINTS.

DESIGN **IVO DRPIC m. of architecture**
10101 SOUTHWEST FRWY, SUITE 104
HOUSTON, TX. 77074 TEL 713 772.0758

# LEARNING TO SKETCH FAST AND EFFECTIVELY

THERE ARE SEVERAL APPROACHES FOR LEARNING HOW TO SKETCH FAST AND EFFECTIVELY.

THE FIRST THING THE SKETCHER HAS TO DO IS TO LOOSEN HIS OR HER HAND. THIS CAN PARTLY BE ACCOMPLISHED THROUGH THE FOLLOWING EXERCISES.

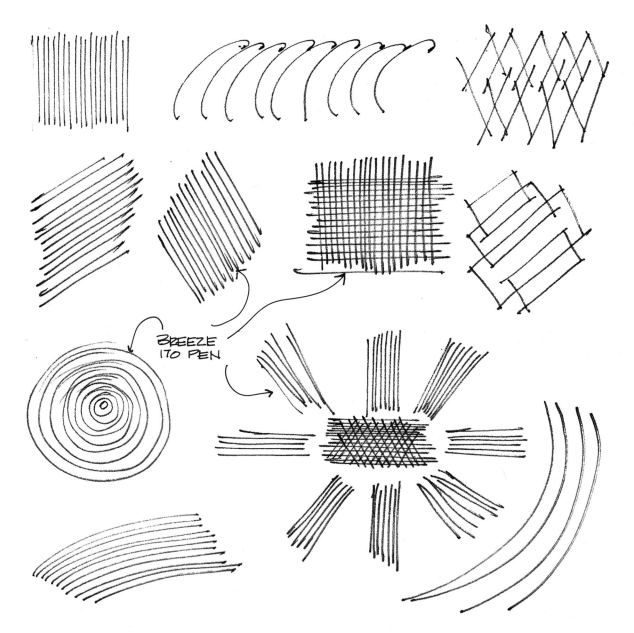

BREEZE
170 PEN

TRY THESE PEN STROKES SEVERAL TIMES. BE SURE TO DO THEM FASTER EACH TIME.

START SKETCHING VERY SIMPLE GEOMETRIC FIGURES.

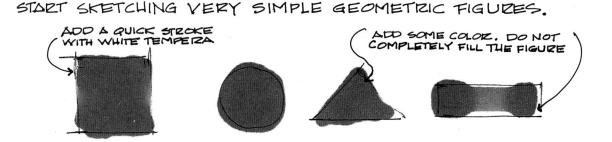

ADD A QUICK STROKE
WITH WHITE TEMPERA

ADD SOME COLOR. DO NOT
COMPLETELY FILL THE FIGURE

SKETCH AND REPEAT EACH FIGURE AT LEAST FIFTY TIMES.
TRY THE SAME APPROACH WITH GEOMETRIC SOLIDS, AS
SHOWN.

NO PROBLEM IF THE COLOR GOES OUT
OF THE LIMITS

TO THE SAME SOLIDS ALSO ADD SOME SHADOWS, AS SHOWN.
NOTE: DO NOT DEFINE THE SHADOWS; KEEP THE FIGURE
LOOSE, BECAUSE AT THIS MOMENT YOU PROBABLY DO NOT
HAVE A DEEP KNOWLEDGE OF HOW TO MAKE SHADOWS.

REINFORCE THE EDGES WITH
A SHARPIE PEN

KEEP THE EDGE OF THE
SHADOW LOOSE

APPLY VERTICAL STROKES OF COLOR

LET'S GO ONE STEP FURTHER.

TAKE ONE OF THE SOLIDS THAT YOU WERE WORKING WITH AND PROCEED AS FOLLOWS:

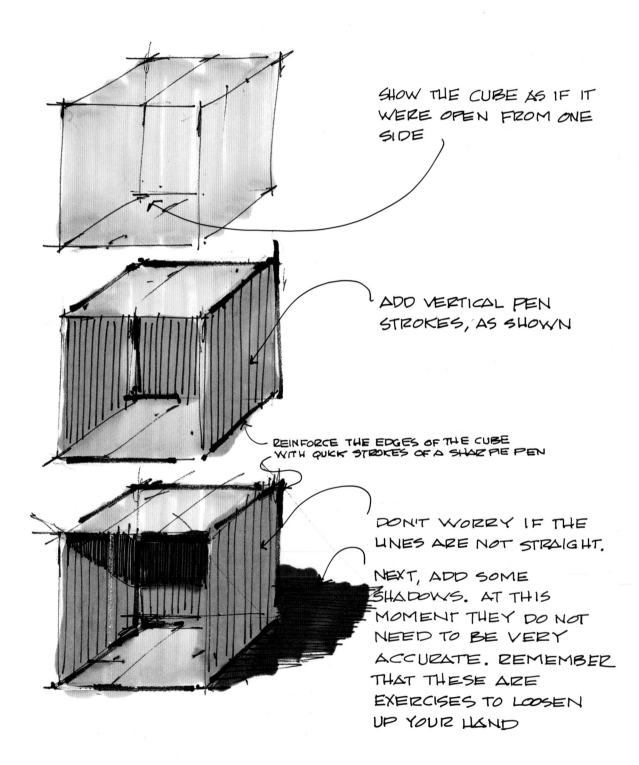

SHOW THE CUBE AS IF IT WERE OPEN FROM ONE SIDE

ADD VERTICAL PEN STROKES, AS SHOWN

REINFORCE THE EDGES OF THE CUBE WITH QUICK STROKES OF A SHARPIE PEN

DON'T WORRY IF THE LINES ARE NOT STRAIGHT.

NEXT, ADD SOME SHADOWS. AT THIS MOMENT THEY DO NOT NEED TO BE VERY ACCURATE. REMEMBER THAT THESE ARE EXERCISES TO LOOSEN UP YOUR HAND

TRY THE SAME
WITH ANY SHAPE.

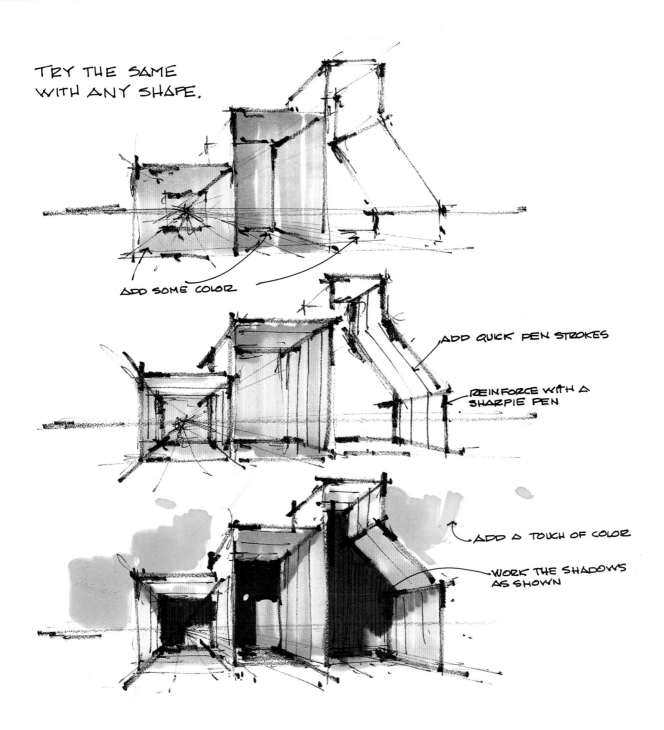

ADD SOME COLOR

ADD QUICK PEN STROKES

REINFORCE WITH A
SHARPIE PEN

ADD A TOUCH OF COLOR

WORK THE SHADOWS
AS SHOWN

KEEP YOUR PEN STROKES LOOSE. DO NOT TRY TO MAKE
PERFECTLY STRAIGHT LINES. THE BEAUTY OF SKETCHES
RELIES PARTLY ON THE SOFTNESS AND IRREGULARITY
OF THE LINES.
NOTE: DO NOT LIMIT YOURSELF TO SKETCHING ONE FORM.
EXPERIMENT WITH ALL KINDS OF SHAPES.

## MATERIALS AND EQUIPMENT

THE MATERIALS AND SUPPLIES NEEDED ARE MINIMAL AND CONSIST MAINLY OF THE FOLLOWING:

1.  SKETCH PAPER, PREFERABLY IN ROLLS. I PREFER WHITE PAPER BECAUSE IT REPRODUCES BETTER THAN YELLOW PAPER IN PHOTOS. MOST BRANDS OF PAPER ARE EXCELLENT.

2.  PADS OF SKETCH PAPER. I USE ART-VEL, WHICH IS A LITTLE THICKER THAN SKETCH PAPER IN ROLLS. SKETCH PADS ARE GOOD FOR WORK IN THE FIELD.

3.  PENS. BASICALLY, I USE TWO KINDS OF PENS: FINE TIP (BREEZE 170 BY EBERHARD FABER) AND OTHER BRANDS, SUCH AS PILOT AND PENTEL. ALL ARE GOOD; YOUR CHOICE IS ONLY A MATTER OF PERSONAL PREFERENCE.
    FOR HEAVIER PEN STROKES (LINE REINFORCEMENT), I USE THE SHARPIE PEN BY SANFORD.

4.  COLOR MARKERS. BEROL PRISMACOLOR IS VERY GOOD BECAUSE THERE ARE TWO DIFFERENT TIPS IN THE SAME MARKER.
    OTHER BRANDS, SUCH AS PANTONE, MAGIC MARKER, AND DESIGN (EBERHARD FABER) ARE ALSO VERY GOOD.

5.  TEMPERA PAINT. I USE DIFFERENT COLORS WITH A THIN BRUSH FOR HIGHLIGHTING.

## ORGANIZING SPACE WITH PERSPECTIVES AND PLANS

IN ORDER TO SHOW THREE-DIMENSIONAL SPACES ON A
TWO-DIMENSIONAL SURFACE, WHICH IS WHAT YOU DO IN
SKETCHING, YOU NEED TO MASTER PERSPECTIVES AND
PLANS. THIS SECTION SHOWS HOW TO ORGANIZE SPACE
USING FOUR DIFFERENT METHODS THAT WORK VERY WELL
IN INTERIOR DESIGN WORK:

- ONE-POINT PERSPECTIVE
- TWO-POINT PERSPECTIVE
- AXONOMETRIC VIEWS
- FOLD-OUT PLANS

THE METHODS SHOWN HERE HAVE BEEN DEVELOPED
FOR ACHIEVING PROFESSIONAL RESULTS WITH A MINIMUM
OF SCIENCE AND A MAXIMUM OF SPEED.

## ONE-POINT PERSPECTIVE

THE SIMPLEST OF ALL PERSPECTIVES IS THE ONE-POINT. IT IS
THE BASIS OF THE OTHER TWO PERSPECTIVES SHOWN ON
THE PAGES AHEAD: TWO-POINT AND AXONOMETRIC.

DOING ONE-POINT POINT PERSPECTIVE IS VERY SIMPLE.

DRAW A HORIZON LINE (HL).

LOCATE THE VANISHING POINT (VP).

DRAW VERTICAL LINES TO INDICATE THE ELEVATION OF
THE SPACE YOU ARE GOING TO REPRESENT.
USE AS A GUIDE THE HEIGHT OF A PERSON, EYEBALLING
APPROXIMATELY 5'-6"
FROM THE HORIZON
LINE TO A FLOOR LINE
AND 3' FROM THE
HORIZON LINE TO A
CEILING LINE, AS
SHOWN.
NOW RADIATE DIAGONAL
LINES FROM THE
VANISHING POINT

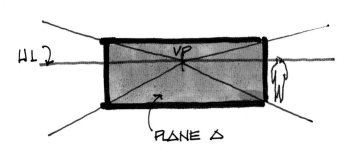

THROUGH THE FOUR CORNERS OF THE PLANE (ELEVATION) "A."
EYEBALL THE DEPTH OF THE SPACE AND INDICATE IT BY
DRAWING A LARGER PLANE AS SHOWN.

YOU NOW HAVE A
PERSPECTIVE VIEW
THAT SHOWS SIDE
WALLS, FLOOR, AND
CEILING.

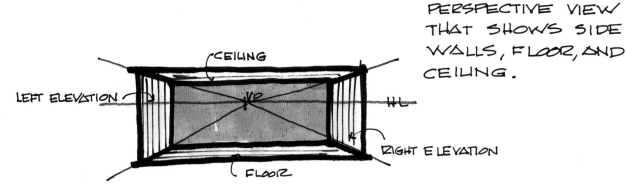

## VARIATIONS ON ONE-POINT PERSPECTIVE

IT IS EASY TO OBTAIN VARIATIONS OF A ONE-POINT PERSPECTIVE. JUST RELOCATE THE VANISHING POINT (VP) ALONG THE HORIZON LINE (HL) AS SHOWN.

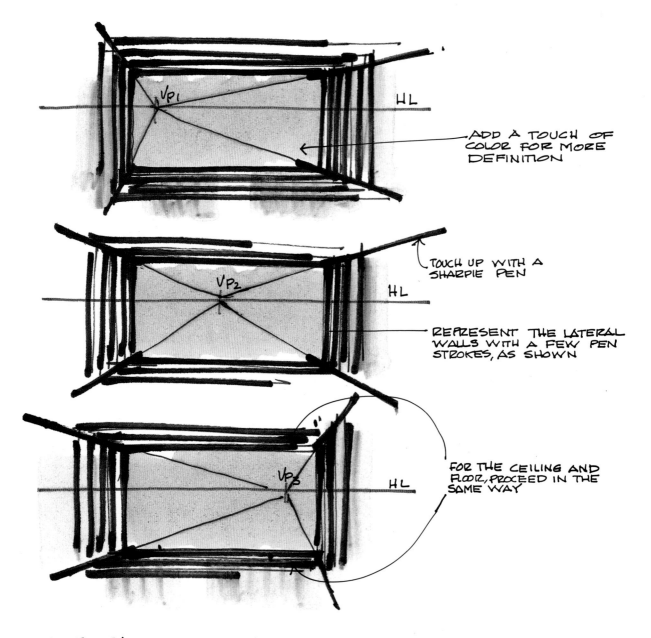

ADD A TOUCH OF COLOR FOR MORE DEFINITION

TOUCH UP WITH A SHARPIE PEN

REPRESENT THE LATERAL WALLS WITH A FEW PEN STROKES, AS SHOWN

FOR THE CEILING AND FLOOR, PROCEED IN THE SAME WAY

NOTE: THIS BASIC ARCHITECTURAL SPACE DOES NOT SHOW DOORS, WINDOWS, OR FURNITURE. THE POSITIONING OF THESE ELEMENTS IS EASY AND WILL BE EXPLAINED LATER.

THE SAME PRINCIPLE APPLIES
TO TALLER SPACES.

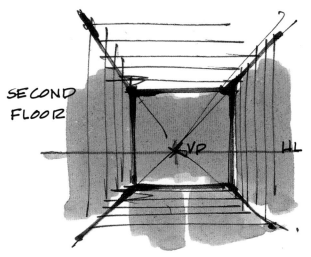

SECOND
FLOOR

VP      HL

FOLLOW THE SAME STEPS
AGAIN:

DRAW THE HORIZON LINE (HL).
LOCATE THE VANISHING POINT (VP).
ESTIMATE ROUGHLY THE HEIGHT
OF THE SPACE (MAINTAIN 5'-6")
FROM FLOOR TO HORIZON LINE
(HL).

COMPLETE THE HEIGHT OF THE
ELEVATION.

RADIATE LINES THROUGH THE
FOUR CORNERS.

DEFINE THE SPACE BY
DRAWING A FEW PEN
STROKES HORIZONTALLY
AND VERTICALLY.

FOR TALLER SPACES (ABOVE
2 STORIES) JUST FOLLOW
THE PROCEDURE AS
SHOWN IN THE FIGURES
AT RIGHT.

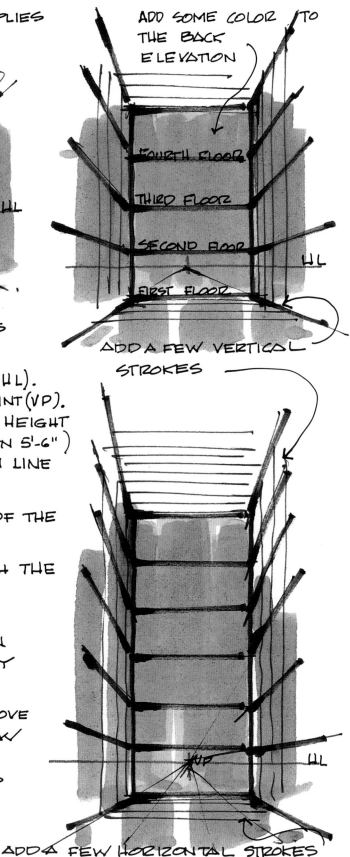

ADD SOME COLOR TO
THE BACK
ELEVATION

FOURTH FLOOR

THIRD FLOOR

SECOND FLOOR      HL

FIRST FLOOR

ADD A FEW VERTICAL
STROKES

VP      HL

ADD A FEW HORIZONTAL STROKES

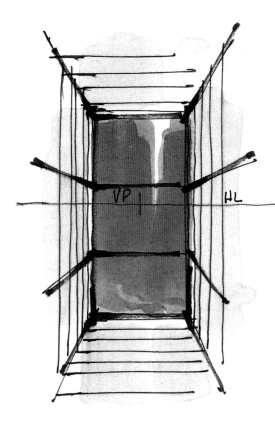

IMPORTANT POINTS TO REMEMBER:

ALWAYS TRY TO EYEBALL THE PROPORTION NEEDED WITHOUT THE USE OF INSTRUMENTS SUCH AS RULERS.

PRACTICE PUTTING THE ELEMENTS IN PROPORTION OR SCALE. WITH PRACTICE, YOU WILL DEVELOP A KEEN EYE.

BY MOVING OR RELOCATING THE HORIZON LINE AND THE VANISHING POINT, YOU CAN CREATE OTHER KINDS OF VIEWS AND SPACES.

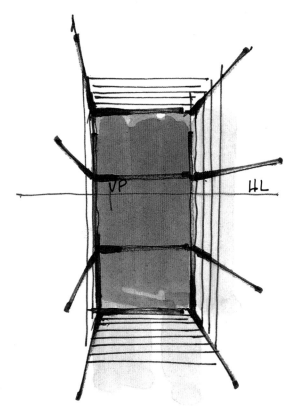

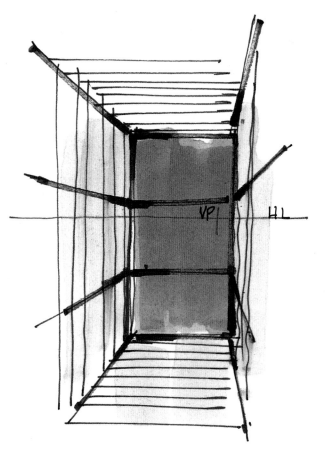

## MORE VARIATIONS

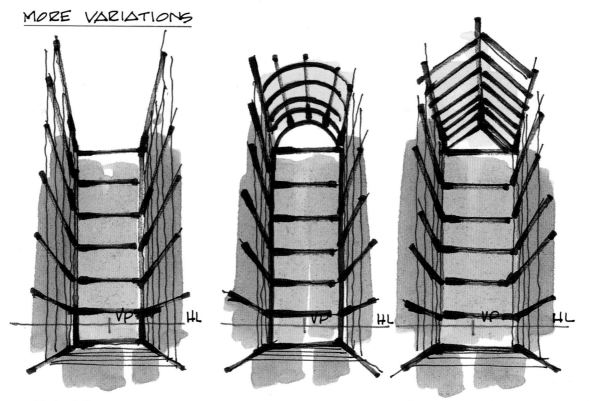

THE VARIATIONS OF VIEWS ARE COUNTLESS. HERE ARE SOME EXAMPLES. NOTICE THE DIFFERENT CEILING SHAPES.

BY CHANGING THE VANISHING POINTS YOU WILL HAVE THESE NEW VIEWPOINTS.

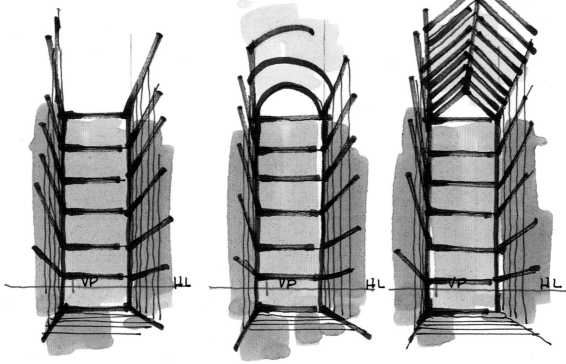

## TWO-POINT PERSPECTIVE

TWO-POINT PERSPECTIVE IS ESPECIALLY EFFECTIVE IN SHOWING INTERIOR SPACES. IN FACT, IT IS THE MOST IMPORTANT PERSPECTIVE FOR INTERIORS WORK.

IN GIVING FORM TO INTERIOR SPACES, TWO-POINT PERSPECTIVE ESSENTIALLY INVERTS THE PROCESS USED BY ARCHITECTS TO DELINEATE EXTERIOR VIEWS OF BUILDINGS.

TWO-POINT PERSPECTIVE REQUIRES THAT YOU PUT YOUR IMAGINATION TO WORK AND THAT YOU PRACTICE MANY CONFIGURATIONS.

IVO DRPIC

WHEREAS ONE-POINT PERSPECTIVE INVOLVES A SINGLE VANISHING POINT, TWO-POINT PERSPECTIVE DEPENDS ON ESTABLISHING TWO VANISHING POINTS.

TO BEGIN, FORGET ALL FORMULAS AND PRINCIPLES OF GEOMETRY. FREE YOUR MIND AND FOLLOW THE SIMPLE STEPS SHOWN BELOW.

DRAW A HORIZON LINE.

ESTABLISH A PERPENDICULAR LINE AS SHOWN.

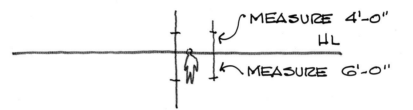

LOCATE VP1 AND VP2 BY DRAWING LINES FROM THE TOP AND BOTTOM OF THE PERPENDICULAR TO THE ENDS OF THE HORIZON LINE. EXTEND THOSE LINES WELL BEYOND THE PERPENDICULAR LINE.

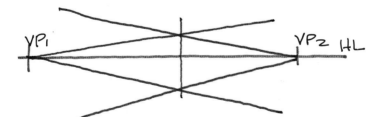

DRAW TWO MORE PERPENDICULARS AS SHOWN.

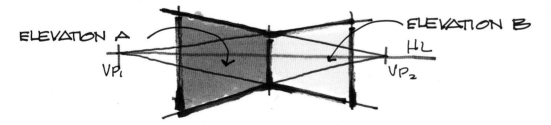

YOU HAVE CREATED TWO ELEVATIONS, A AND B, WHICH ARE THE BASIS OF THE NEXT STAGES OF SKETCHING OR SPATIAL MANIPULATION.

IF YOU RELOCATE THE VANISHING POINT VP₁ AS SHOWN, THE RESULT WILL BE A CHANGED VIEWPOINT.

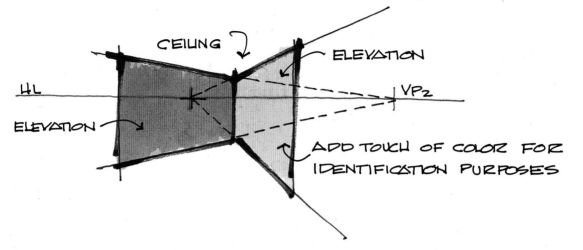

IF YOU RELOCATE VP₁ TO YET A DIFFERENT POSITION, HERE IS WHAT HAPPENS.

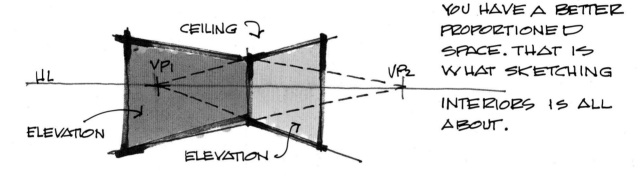

YOU HAVE A BETTER PROPORTIONED SPACE. THAT IS WHAT SKETCHING

INTERIORS IS ALL ABOUT.

TRY RELOCATING THE OTHER VANISHING POINT, VP₂

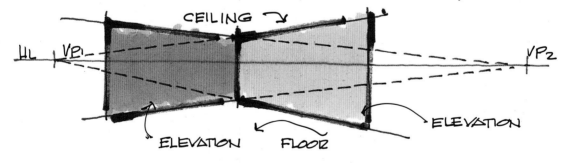

YOU CAN MOVE THE VANISHING POINTS ALMOST INFINITELY. WITH PRACTICE, YOU WILL NEED ONLY A FEW OF THESE SCHEMES IN ORDER TO DETERMINE THE CORRECT VIEW. I STRONGLY DISCOURAGE THE USE OF PERSPECTIVE CHARTS. IF YOU BECOME RELIANT ON THEM, YOUR SKETCHING WILL TEND TO BECOME TOO MECHANICAL.

NOW, LET'S CHANGE THE HEIGHT OF THE INTERIOR SPACE.

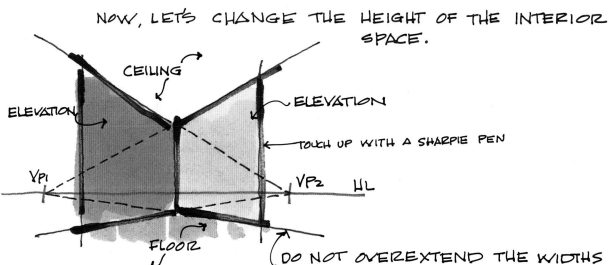

CEILING

ELEVATION

ELEVATION

TOUCH UP WITH A SHARPIE PEN

VP1

VP2    HL

FLOOR

DO NOT OVEREXTEND THE WIDTHS OF THE ELEVATIONS. IF YOU DO, THE SPACE WILL LOOK DISTORTED AND AWKWARD. AT ALL TIMES, BE SURE TO KEEP THE PROPORTIONS BASED ON HUMAN PROPORTION.

LET'S SEE WHAT HAPPENS WHEN THE VANISHING POINTS CHANGE.

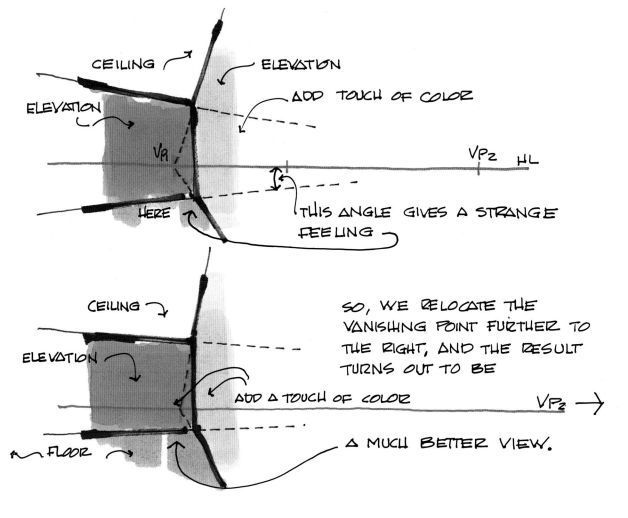

CEILING    ELEVATION

ELEVATION

ADD TOUCH OF COLOR

VP1

VP2    HL

HERE

THIS ANGLE GIVES A STRANGE FEELING

CEILING

ELEVATION

ADD A TOUCH OF COLOR

FLOOR

SO, WE RELOCATE THE VANISHING POINT FURTHER TO THE RIGHT, AND THE RESULT TURNS OUT TO BE

VP2 →

A MUCH BETTER VIEW.

PRACTICE RELOCATING THE VANISHING POINTS UNTIL YOU FEEL
COMFORTABLE WITH THE VIEW. IT TAKES ONLY A FEW
MINUTES. FOR NOW, MAKE YOUR SKETCHES NO LARGER
THAN THE SIZE SHOWN.
WHEN YOU FIND THE RIGHT SKETCH (VIEW, PROPORTION,
FEELING), THEN START WORKING WITH THE ARCHITECTURAL
ELEMENTS. HERE ARE SOME POSSIBILITIES.

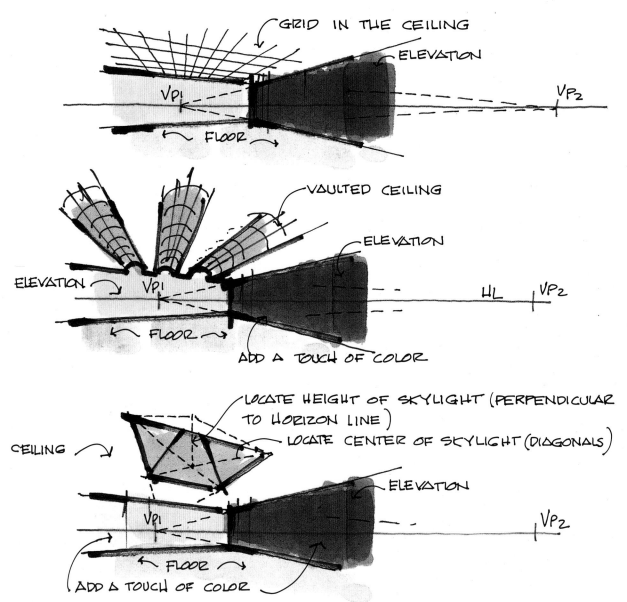

LOCATE DOORS, WINDOWS, AND OTHER ELEMENTS BY APPLYING
THE CONCEPT OF PROPORTION IN RELATION TO THE HUMAN
FIGURE AND THE ARCHITECTURAL PROGRAM.
THE ALTERNATIVES AND DESIGN ARE YOURS.

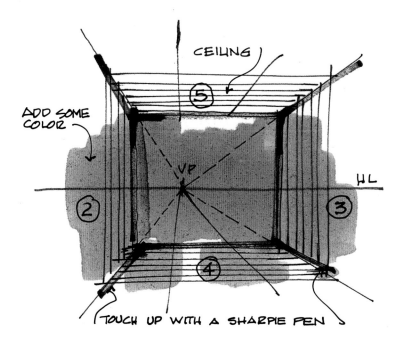

CEILING

⑤

ADD SOME
COLOR

VP

HL

② ③

④

TOUCH UP WITH A SHARPIE PEN

NOW THAT YOU HAVE AN
IDEA OF ONE - AND
TWO - POINT PERSPECTIVE,
BEGIN PRACTICING THIS:

DRAW FREEHAND ANY
SIMPLE SPACE. START
BY MAKING A SERIES
OF PARALLEL LINES IN
PLANES 2, 3, 4 AND 5
AS SHOWN.

DO NOT WORRY IF THE
LINES ARE NOT PERFECT.
THAT IS PART OF THE
SKETCH.

START GIVING A SENSE OF DEPTH.

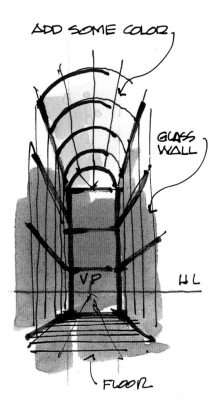

ADD SOME COLOR

GLASS
WALL

VP

HL

FLOOR

CEILING

VP

HL

ADD SOME COLOR

FLOOR

SHOW SOME RADIAL LINES
ORIGINATING FROM THE
VANISHING POINT.

EACH TIME, TRY TO SKETCH A
SPACE THAT IS A LITTLE MORE
COMPLICATED THAN THE PREVIOUS
ONE.

# PERSPECTIVE PRACTICE EXAMPLES

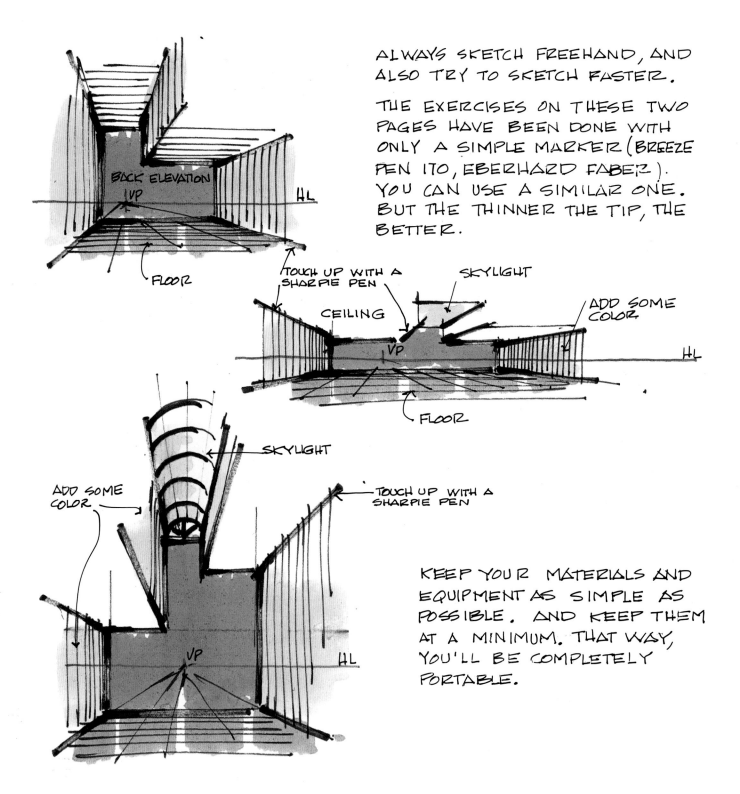

ALWAYS SKETCH FREEHAND, AND ALSO TRY TO SKETCH FASTER.

THE EXERCISES ON THESE TWO PAGES HAVE BEEN DONE WITH ONLY A SIMPLE MARKER (BREEZE PEN 170, EBERHARD FABER). YOU CAN USE A SIMILAR ONE. BUT THE THINNER THE TIP, THE BETTER.

BACK ELEVATION
VP
HL
FLOOR

TOUCH UP WITH A SHARPIE PEN
CEILING
SKYLIGHT
ADD SOME COLOR
VP
HL
FLOOR

SKYLIGHT
ADD SOME COLOR
TOUCH UP WITH A SHARPIE PEN
VP
HL

KEEP YOUR MATERIALS AND EQUIPMENT AS SIMPLE AS POSSIBLE. AND KEEP THEM AT A MINIMUM. THAT WAY, YOU'LL BE COMPLETELY PORTABLE.

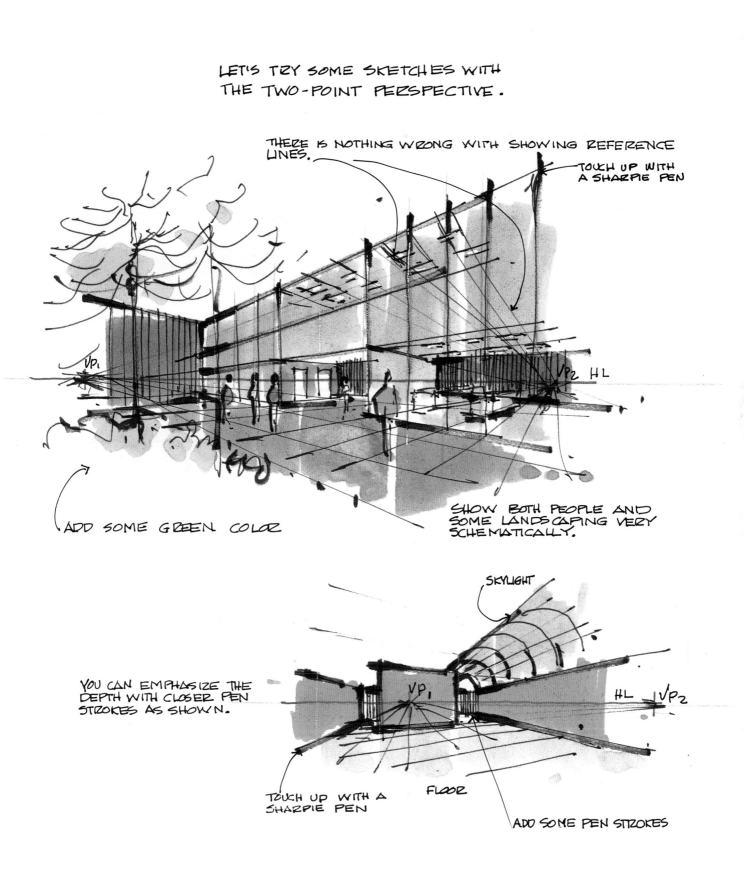

LET'S TRY SOME SKETCHES WITH
THE TWO-POINT PERSPECTIVE.

THERE IS NOTHING WRONG WITH SHOWING REFERENCE
LINES.

TOUCH UP WITH
A SHARPIE PEN

VP₁

VP₂  HL

ADD SOME GREEN COLOR

SHOW BOTH PEOPLE AND
SOME LANDSCAPING VERY
SCHEMATICALLY.

SKYLIGHT

YOU CAN EMPHASIZE THE
DEPTH WITH CLOSER PEN
STROKES AS SHOWN.

VP₁

HL  VP₂

TOUCH UP WITH A
SHARPIE PEN

FLOOR

ADD SOME PEN STROKES

# AXONOMETRIC VIEW

THE AXONOMETRIC VIEW IS ANOTHER METHOD, OR WAY, TO REPRESENT AN ARCHITECTURAL SPACE. THE AXONOMETRIC SKETCH IS A VERY SIMPLE PROJECTION FROM A FLOOR PLAN OR SECTION IN WHICH ALL PARALLEL LINES IN THE SPACE ARE SHOWN PARALLEL. (THIS DIFFERS FROM PERSPECTIVES, IN WHICH ALL THE PARALLELS CONVERGE INTO ONE, TWO, OR EVEN THREE VANISHING POINTS.

ANOTHER ADVANTAGE OF AXONOMETRIC VIEWS IS THAT ALL THREE DIMENSIONS ARE SHOWN AT THE SAME SCALE.

FROM THE EXISTING FLOOR PLAN, JUST PROJECT LINES AS SHOWN. APPLY COLOR AFTERWARD.

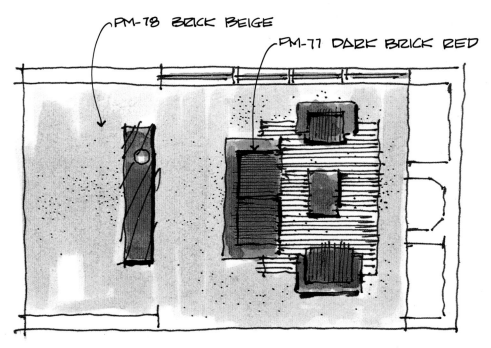

PM-78 BRICK BEIGE

PM-77 DARK BRICK RED

FLOOR PLAN

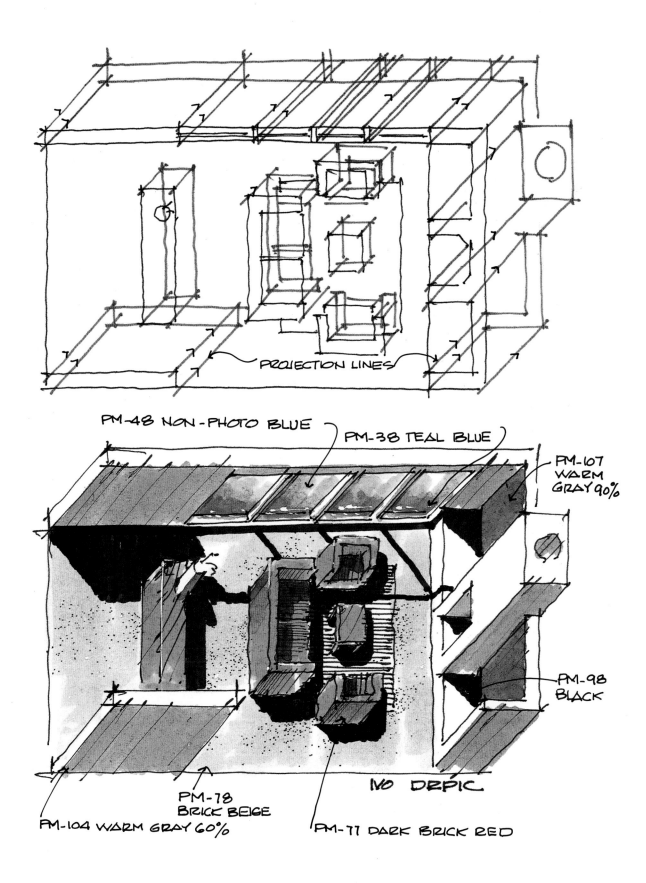

PROJECTION LINES

PM-48 NON-PHOTO BLUE

PM-38 TEAL BLUE

PM-107 WARM GRAY 90%

PM-98 BLACK

PM-78 BRICK BEIGE

IVO DRPIC

PM-104 WARM GRAY 60%

PM-77 DARK BRICK RED

YOU CAN REPRESENT THE SAME SPACE
IN AXONOMETRIC SKETCHES FROM MANY
DIFFERENT POSITIONS, AS SHOWN.

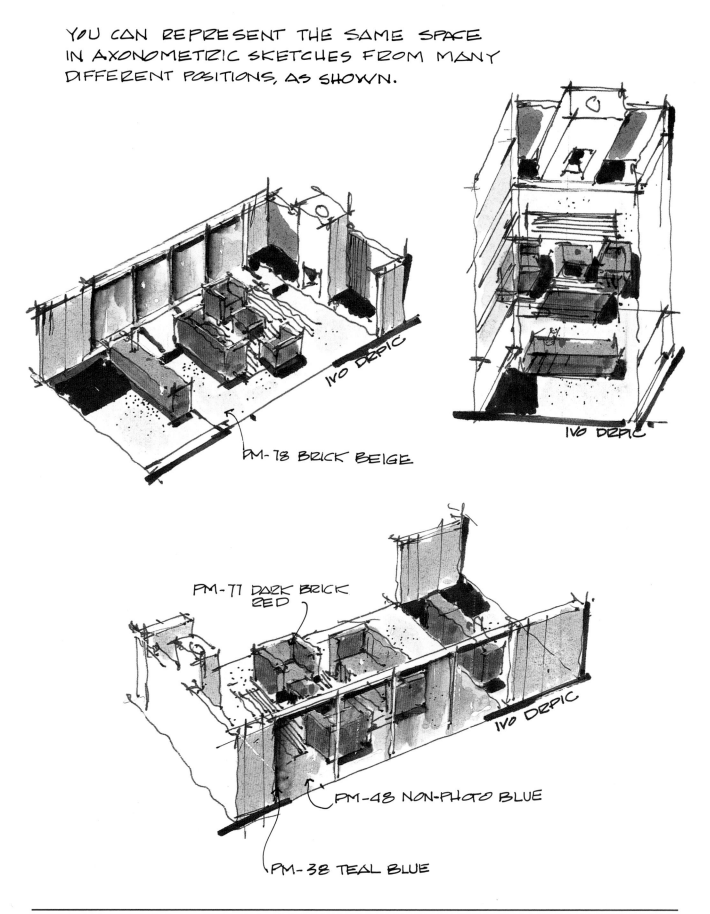

IVO DRPIC

PM-78 BRICK BEIGE

IVO DRPIC

PM-77 DARK BRICK
RED

IVO DRPIC

PM-48 NON-PHOTO BLUE

PM-38 TEAL BLUE

PM-107 WARM GRAY 90%

IVO DRPIC

DON'T BE AFRAID TO SHOW WAVY LINES. THEY ADD
TO THE BEAUTY OF THE SKETCH AND SOFTEN ITS LOOK.

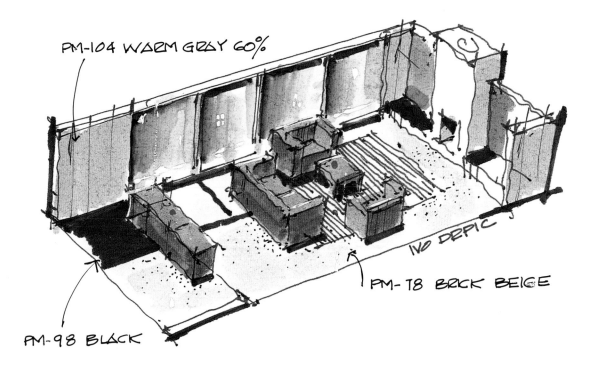

PM-104 WARM GRAY 60%

IVO DRPIC

PM-78 BRICK BEIGE

PM-98 BLACK

# FOLD-OUT PLAN

A USEFUL WAY TO REPRESENT INTERIOR SPACES
IS WITH THE FOLD-OUT PLAN. THIS IS A TRIDIMENSIONAL
DRAWING IN WHICH THE ELEVATIONS ARE "UNFOLDED."
THE ADVANTAGE OF THIS APPROACH IS THAT THE
ELEVATIONS CAN BE RELATED TO THE FLOOR
PLAN WITH GREAT EASE. IT ALSO GIVES AN
IDEA OF THE SPACE AT A GLANCE.

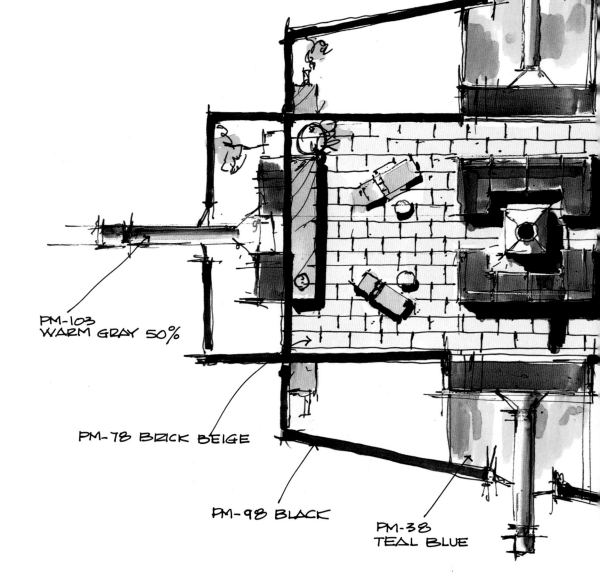

PM-103
WARM GRAY 50%

PM-78 BRICK BEIGE

PM-98 BLACK

PM-38
TEAL BLUE

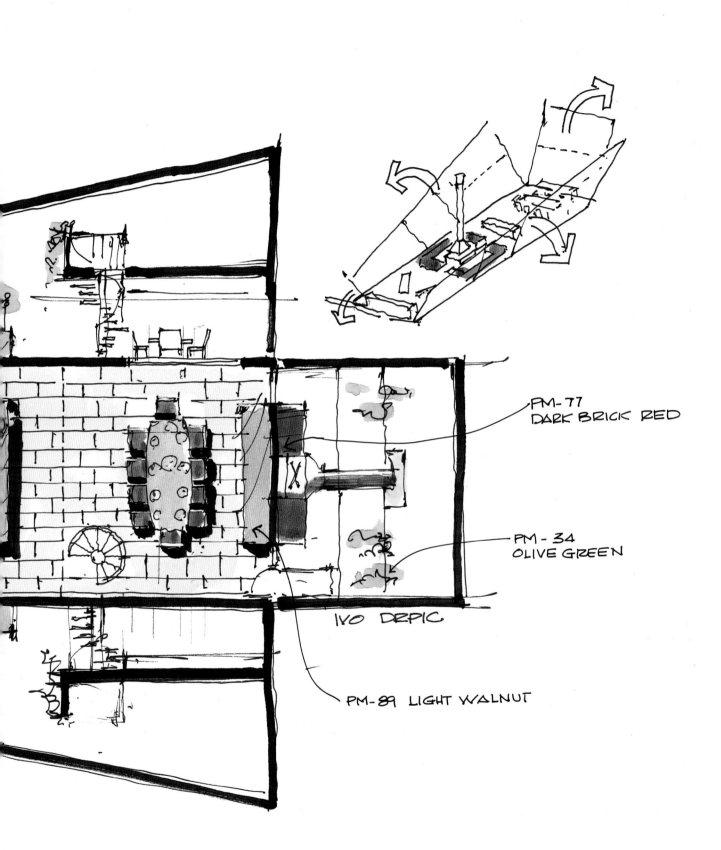

PM-77
DARK BRICK RED

PM-34
OLIVE GREEN

IVO DRPIC

PM-89  LIGHT WALNUT

# The Process of Sketching

## TWENTY-ONE DEMONSTRATIONS

**Presentation Sketch of the Pediatrics Pavilion Lobby, Christ Hospital and Medical Center. Evangelical Health System, Chicago, Illinois**

Architect: The Falick/Klein Partnership, Inc.

Project Manager: Jerry Turner

Senior Project Designer: Ed Huckaby

Project Designer: Diane Osan

Finished sketches of interiors combine a number of individual visual elements: space, light and shadow, simulated surfaces and finishes, and furnishings and entourage. Sketches also present an opportunity to convey a certain look or mood. Techniques for mastering all of these elements are demonstrated in this section.

IVO DRPIC '88

# THUMBNAIL AND CONCEPT SKETCHES

AS THE NAME INDICATES, THESE ARE VERY SMALL
SKETCHES WHICH CAN BE DONE IN A MATTER OF
MINUTES. THEY ARE VERY POWERFUL TOOLS IN THE
PRELIMINARY STAGES OF DESIGN BECAUSE THEY
HELP VISUALIZE THE PROJECT. THESE SKETCHES
REQUIRE SOME SKILL, BUT THEY ARE NOT DIFFICULT
TO MASTER. ALL IT TAKES IS PERSEVERANCE AND
PRACTICE.

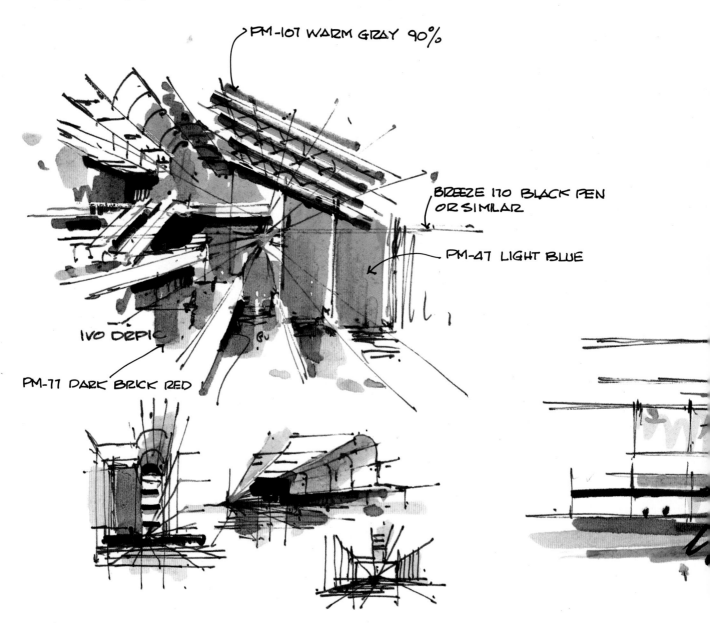

PM-107 WARM GRAY 90%

BREEZE 170 BLACK PEN
OR SIMILAR

PM-47 LIGHT BLUE

IVO ORPIC

PM-77 DARK BRICK RED

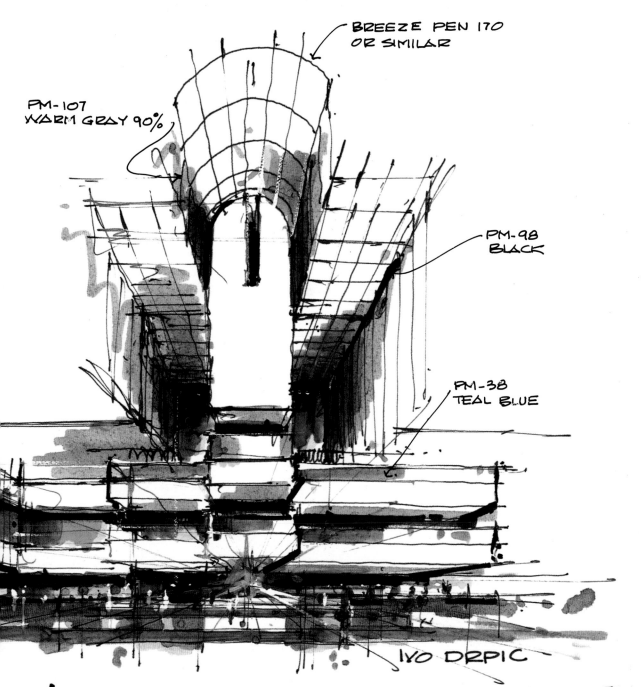

BREEZE PEN 170
OR SIMILAR

PM-107
WARM GRAY 90%

PM-98
BLACK

PM-38
TEAL BLUE

IVO DRPIC

PRELIMINARY STUDIES, ELDORADO COMPLEX, HOUSTON, TEXAS
ARCHITECT: IVO D. DRPIC AND ASSOCIATES

THE PROCESS IS AS FOLLOWS:

START WITH A HORIZONTAL LINE (HL), LOCATE THE
VANISHING POINTS (ONE OR TWO), AND START RADIATING
LINES FROM IT. AS SHOWN, WITH QUICK STROKES,
START SHAPING THE SPACE. PLAY WITH THE LINES
UNTIL YOU HIT THE RIGHT CONFIGURATION. DURING
THIS PROCESS, YOUR MIND WILL START PRODUCING
THE SHAPES OR
CONFIGURATIONS
YOU ARE DOODLING
FOR.

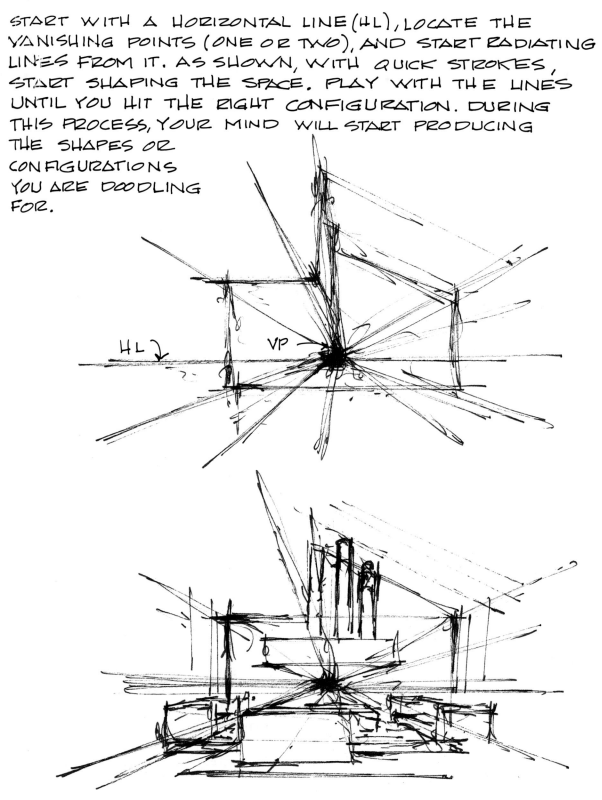

THE KEY IS TO KEEP DOODLING UNTIL YOU ARE
ON THE RIGHT TRACK.

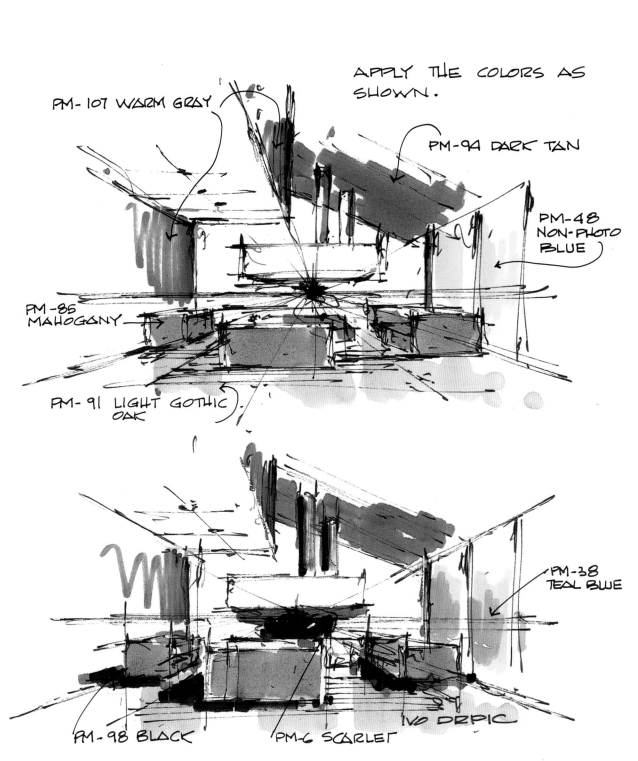

APPLY THE COLORS AS
SHOWN.

PM-107 WARM GRAY

PM-94 DARK TAN

PM-48
NON-PHOTO
BLUE

PM-85
MAHOGANY

PM-91 LIGHT GOTHIC
OAK

PM-38
TEAL BLUE

PM-98 BLACK

PM-6 SCARLET

IVO DRPIC

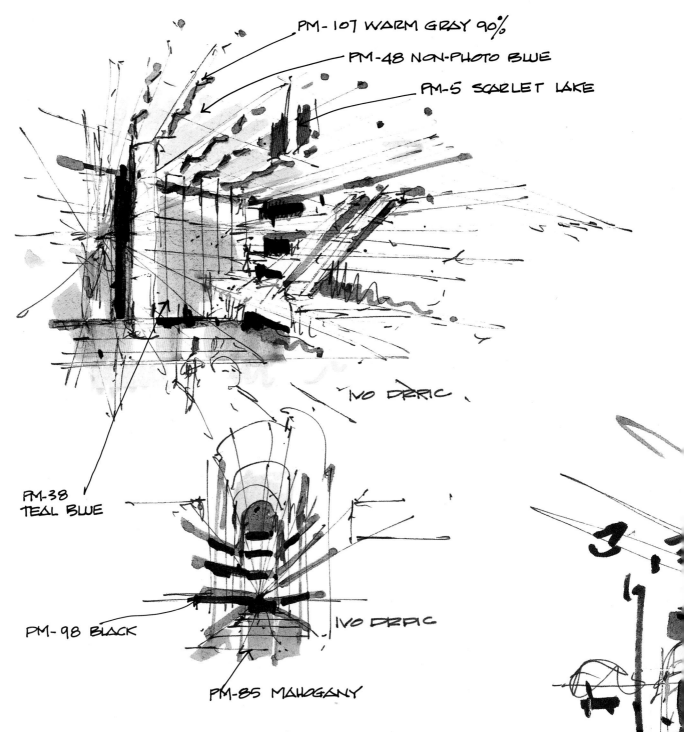

PM-107 WARM GRAY 90%

PM-48 NON-PHOTO BLUE

PM-5 SCARLET LAKE

IVO DRPIC

PM-38
TEAL BLUE

PM-98 BLACK

IVO DRPIC

PM-85 MAHOGANY

PRELIMINARIES. OFFICE BLDG., HOUSTON, TEXAS
ARCHITECT: IVO D. DRPIC AND ASSOCIATES

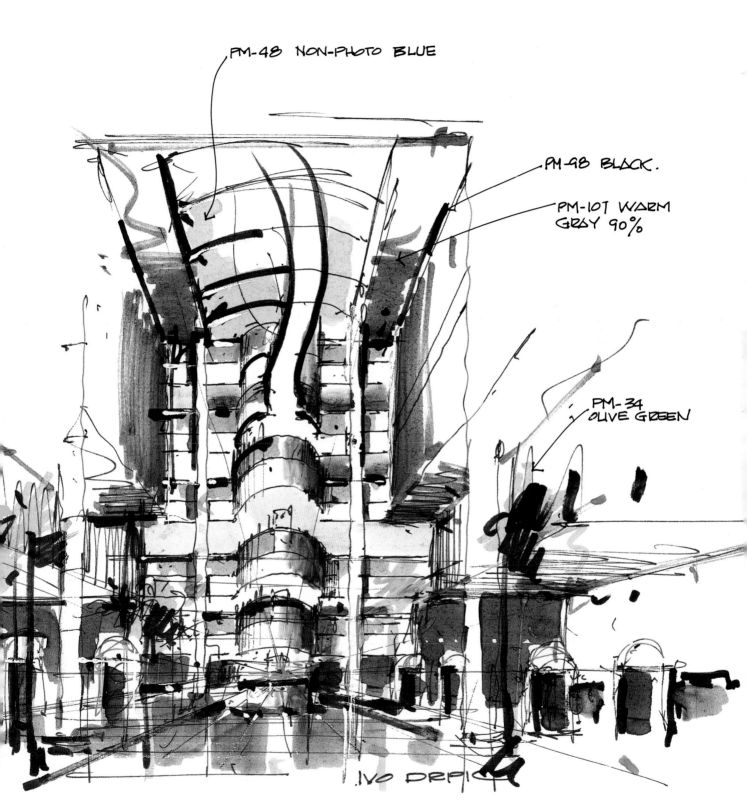

PM-48 NON-PHOTO BLUE

PM-98 BLACK.

PM-107 WARM GRAY 90%

PM-34 OLIVE GREEN

IVO DRPIC

PRELIMINARY. LOBBY, CHRIST HOSPITAL, CHICAGO, ILLINOIS
ARCHITECT : THE FALCK/KLEIN PARTNERSHIP

## SIMPLE SPACE IN ONE-POINT PERSPECTIVE

GIVEN THE FLOOR PLAN AND A SECTION, YOU CAN START EXPLORING FOR THE BEST VIEWS AND BECOME MORE FAMILIAR WITH THE SPACE USING THUMBNAIL SKETCHES (NOT LARGER THAN SHOWN ON THESE TWO PAGES).

VIEWS 1, 2, AND 3 ARE INDICATED IN THE SCHEMATIC FLOOR PLAN.

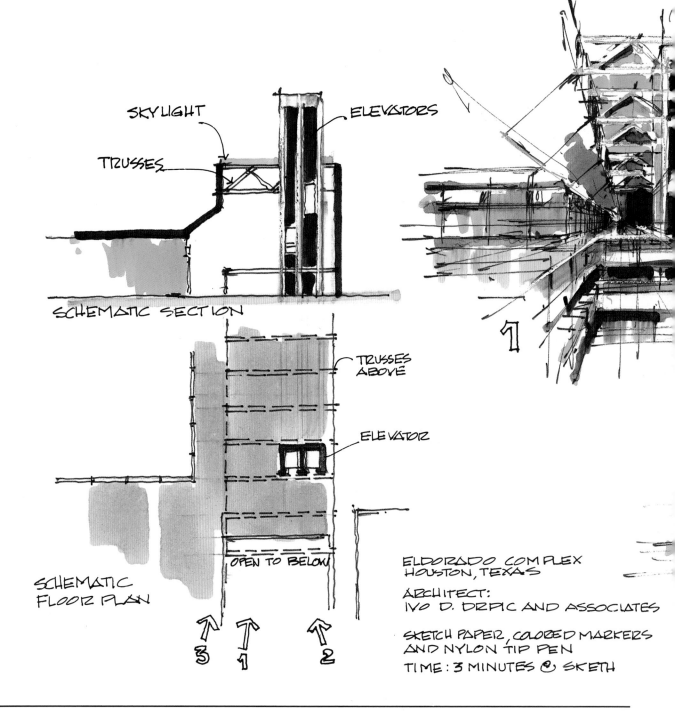

SKYLIGHT

ELEVATORS

TRUSSES

SCHEMATIC SECTION

TRUSSES ABOVE

ELEVATOR

OPEN TO BELOW

SCHEMATIC FLOOR PLAN

3  1  2

ELDORADO COMPLEX
HOUSTON, TEXAS

ARCHITECT:
IVO D. DRPIC AND ASSOCIATES

SKETCH PAPER, COLORED MARKERS
AND NYLON TIP PEN
TIME: 3 MINUTES @ SKETH

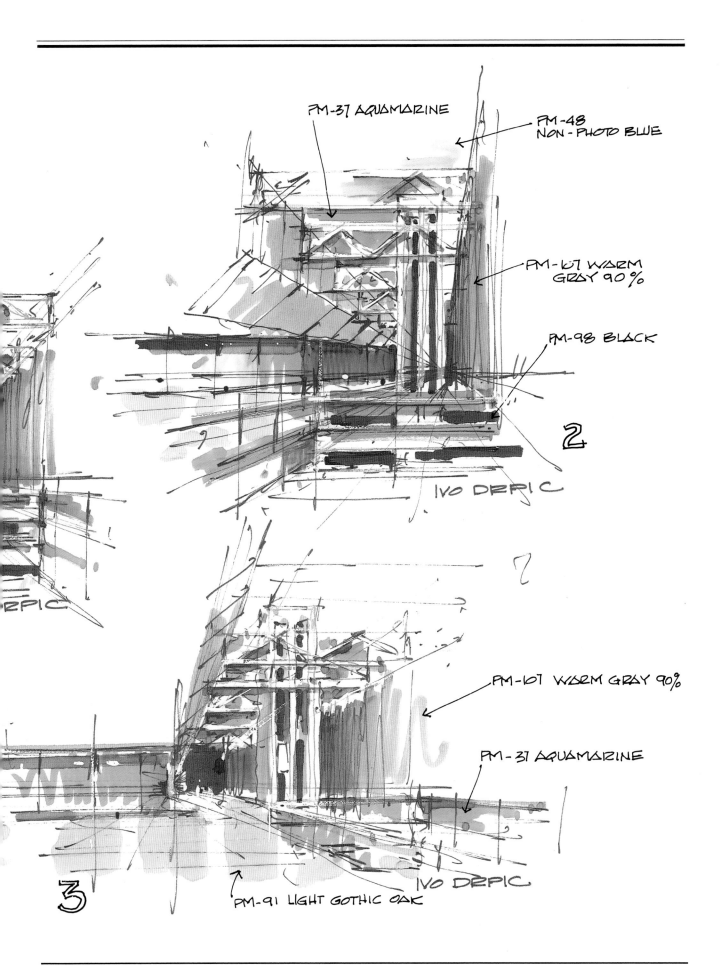

PM-37 AQUAMARINE

PM-48 NON-PHOTO BLUE

PM-107 WARM GRAY 90%

PM-98 BLACK

IVO DRPIC

2

PM-107 WARM GRAY 90%

PM-37 AQUAMARINE

IVO DRPIC

3

PM-91 LIGHT GOTHIC OAK

ONCE YOU HAVE DECIDED WHICH VIEW
BETTER SERVES YOUR PURPOSES,
YOU CAN START SKETCHING ROUGHLY WITH
A BREEZE 170 BLACK PEN (OR SIMILAR).

THE SIZE OF THE SKETCH CAN BE SIMILAR
TO THE ONE SHOWN ON THE NEXT PAGE.
KEEP THE SKETCH VERY LOOSE.

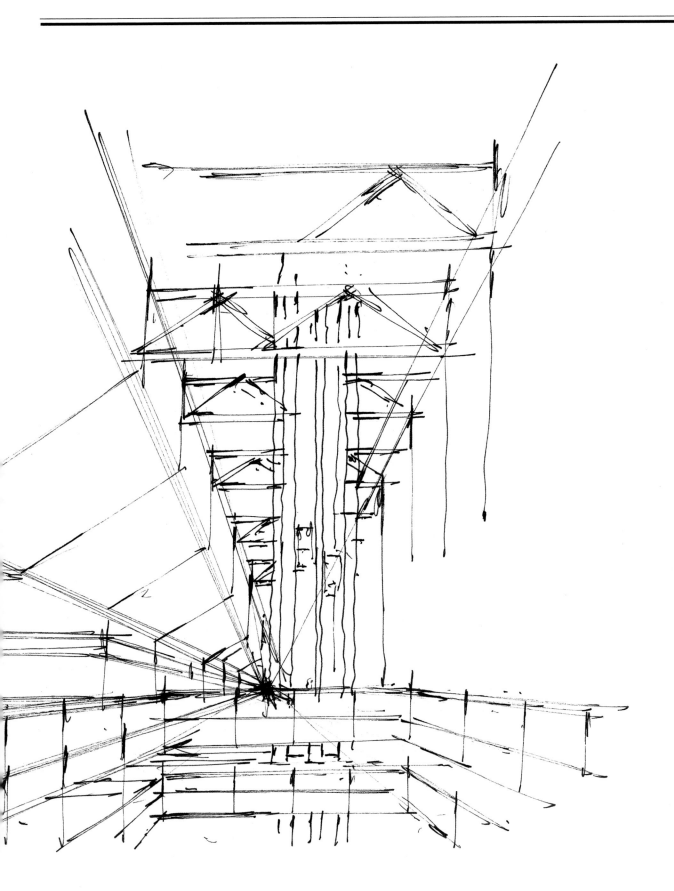

START APPLYNG COLORS AS SHOWN.

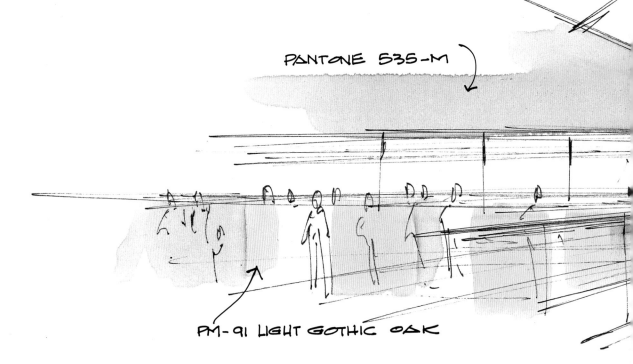

PANTONE 535-M

PM-91 LIGHT GOTHIC OAK

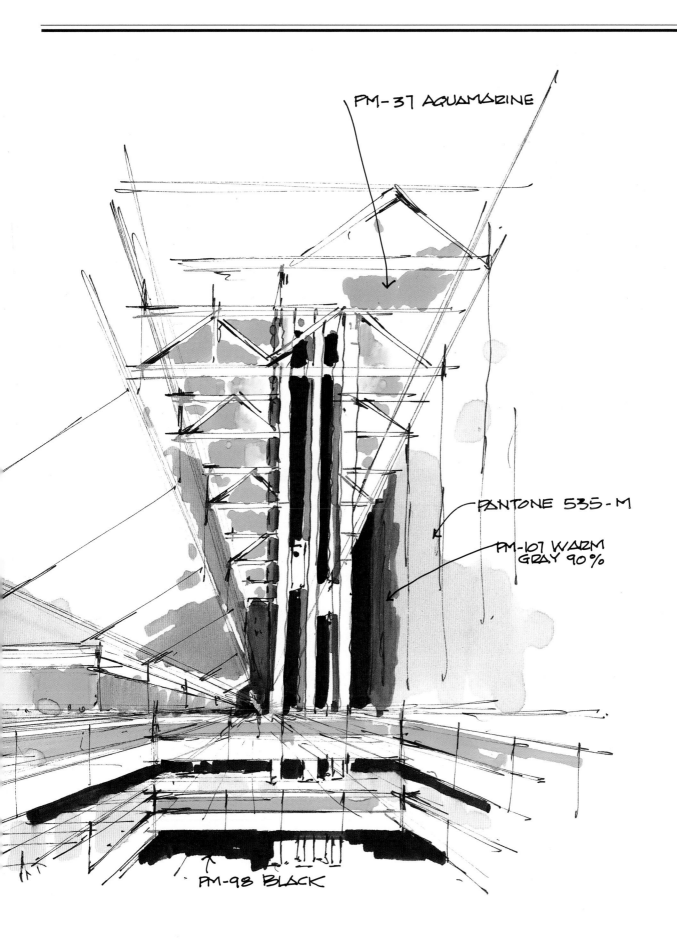

PM-37 AQUAMARINE

PANTONE 535-M

PM-107 WARM
GRAY 90%

PM-98 BLACK

KEEP APPLYNG COLORS
UNTIL YOU ACHIEVE THE
DESIRED RESULTS. BUT
DO NOT OVERWORK IT.

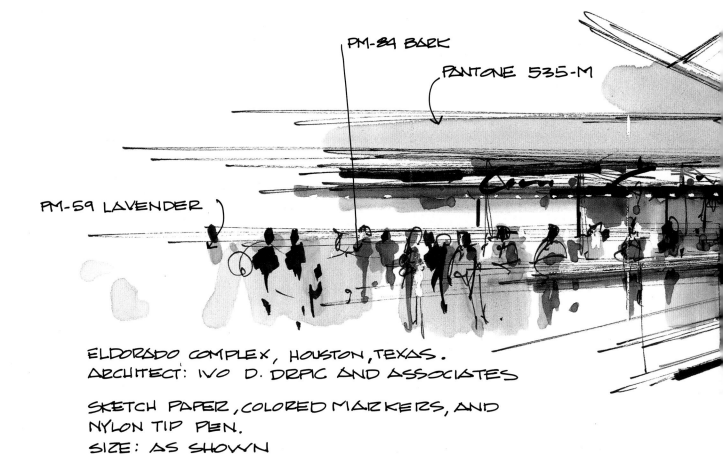

PM-84 BARK

PANTONE 535-M

PM-59 LAVENDER

ELDORADO COMPLEX, HOUSTON, TEXAS.
ARCHITECT: IVO D. DRPIC AND ASSOCIATES

SKETCH PAPER, COLORED MARKERS, AND
NYLON TIP PEN.
SIZE: AS SHOWN
TIME: 10 MINUTES

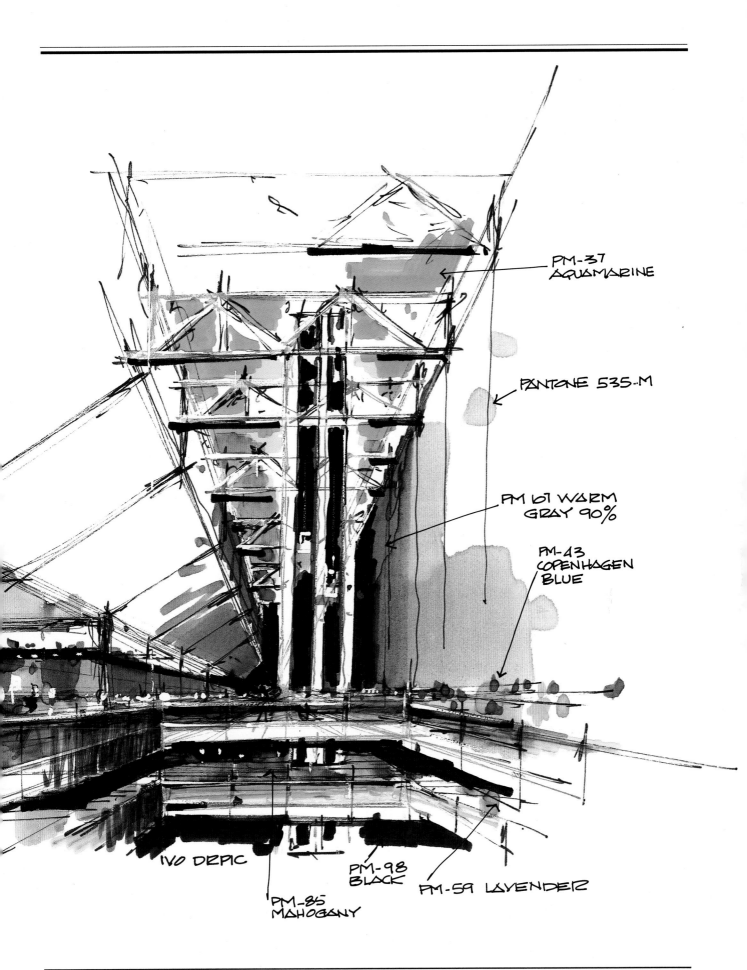

PM-37
AQUAMARINE

PANTONE 535-M

PM 61 WARM
GRAY 90%

PM-43
COPENHAGEN
BLUE

IVO DRPIC

PM-98
BLACK

PM-59 LAVENDER

PM-85
MAHOGANY

# SIMPLE SPACE IN TWO-POINT PERSPECTIVE

BEFORE YOU START SKETCHING THE FINAL VIEW,
EXPLORE DIFFERENT VIEWS WITH THE HELP OF
THUMBNAIL SKETCHES.

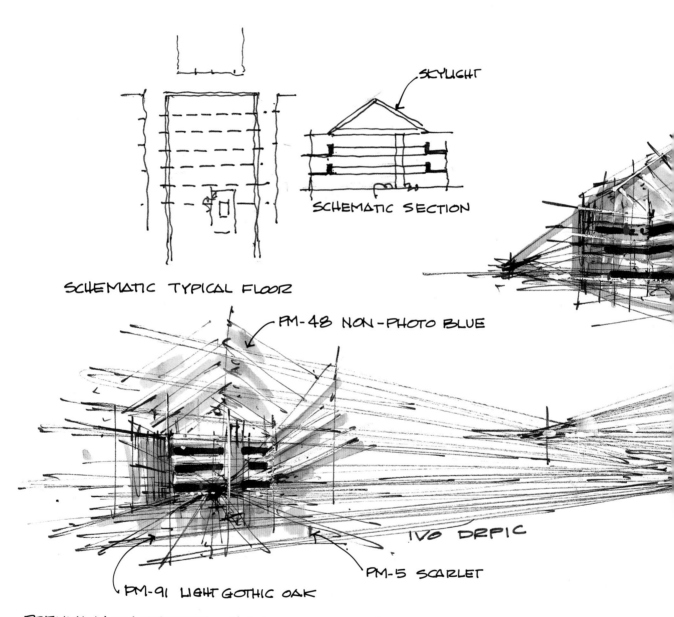

SCHEMATIC SECTION

SCHEMATIC TYPICAL FLOOR

PM-48 NON-PHOTO BLUE

IVO DRPIC

PM-5 SCARLET

PM-91 LIGHT GOTHIC OAK

PRELIMINARY STUDIES. HOLCOMBE OFFICE BLDG., HOUSTON, TEXAS
ARCHITECT: IVO D. DRPIC AND ASSOCIATES.

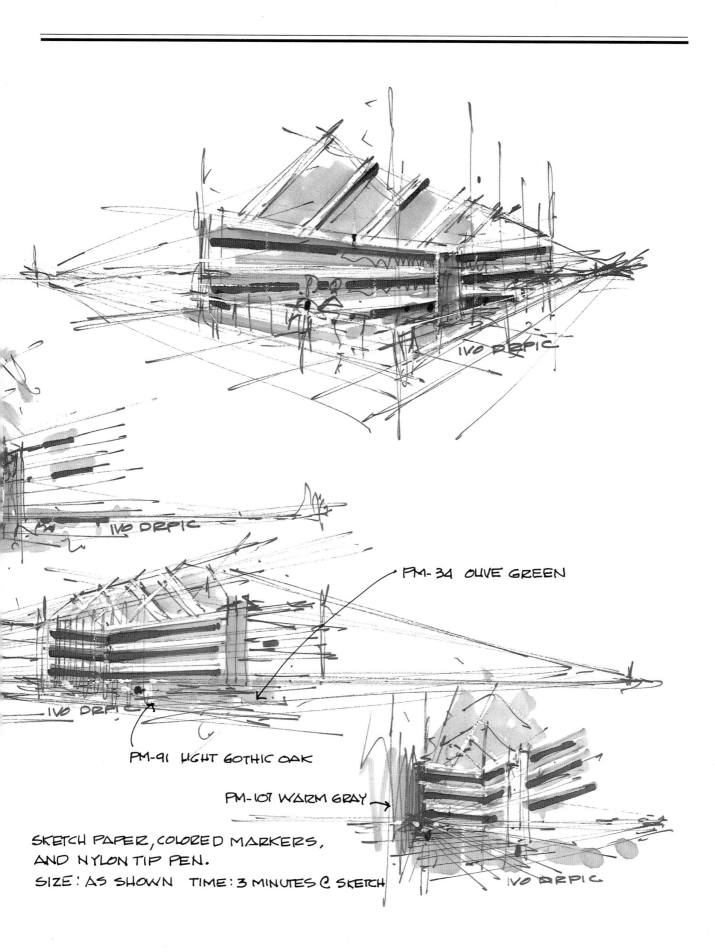

IVO DRPIC

IVO DRPIC

PM-34 OLIVE GREEN

PM-91 LIGHT GOTHIC OAK

PM-107 WARM GRAY →

IVO DRPIC

SKETCH PAPER, COLORED MARKERS,
AND NYLON TIP PEN.
SIZE: AS SHOWN   TIME: 3 MINUTES @ SKETCH

ONCE YOU HAVE DECIDED
WHICH VIEW WORKS BEST,
YOU CAN START A LARGER
SKETCH. KEEP IT VERY
ROUGH, BECAUSE THE REST
OF THE SKETCH IS GOING
TO BE MANIPULATED
THROUGH THE USE OF COLOR.

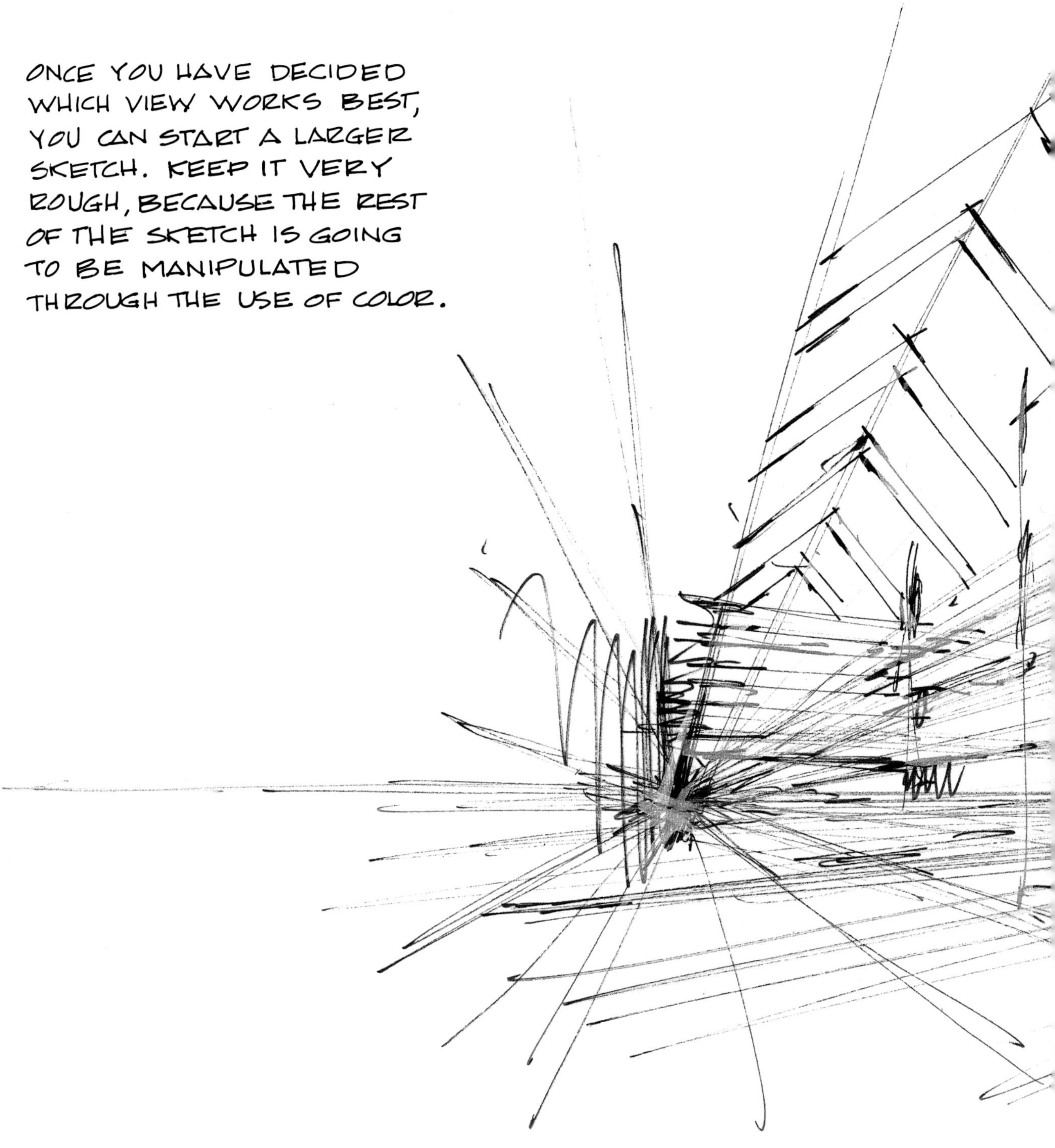

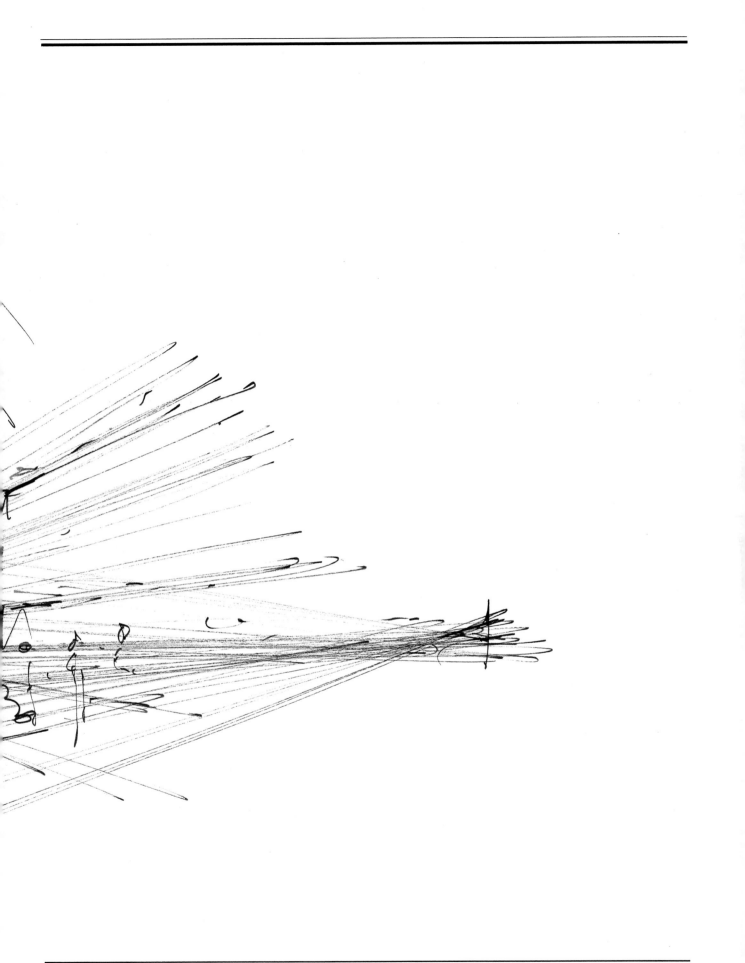

KEEP ADDING COLOR,
AS SHOWN.

PM-107 WARM
GRAY 90%

KEEP PEN STROKES
VERY LOOSE

PM-91
LIGHT GOTHIC OAK

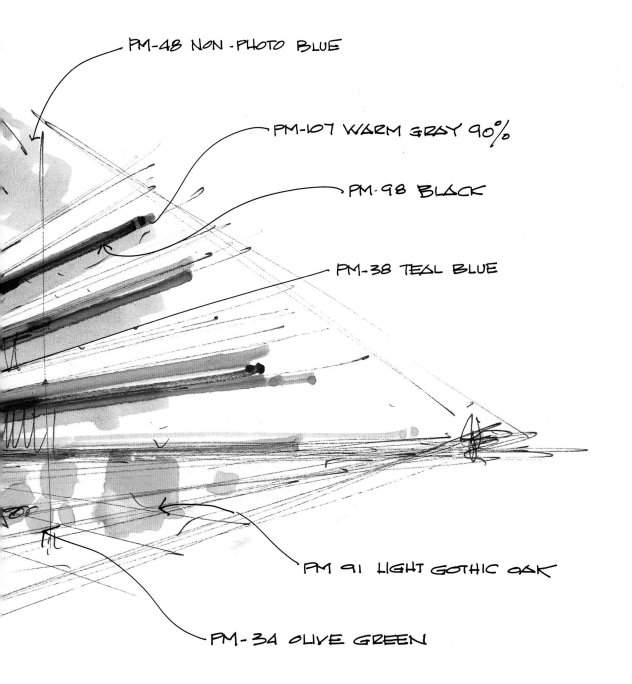

PM-48 NON-PHOTO BLUE

PM-107 WARM GRAY 90%

PM-98 BLACK

PM-38 TEAL BLUE

PM 91 LIGHT GOTHIC OAK

PM-34 OLIVE GREEN

APPLY THE FINAL TOUCHES AS SHOWN.

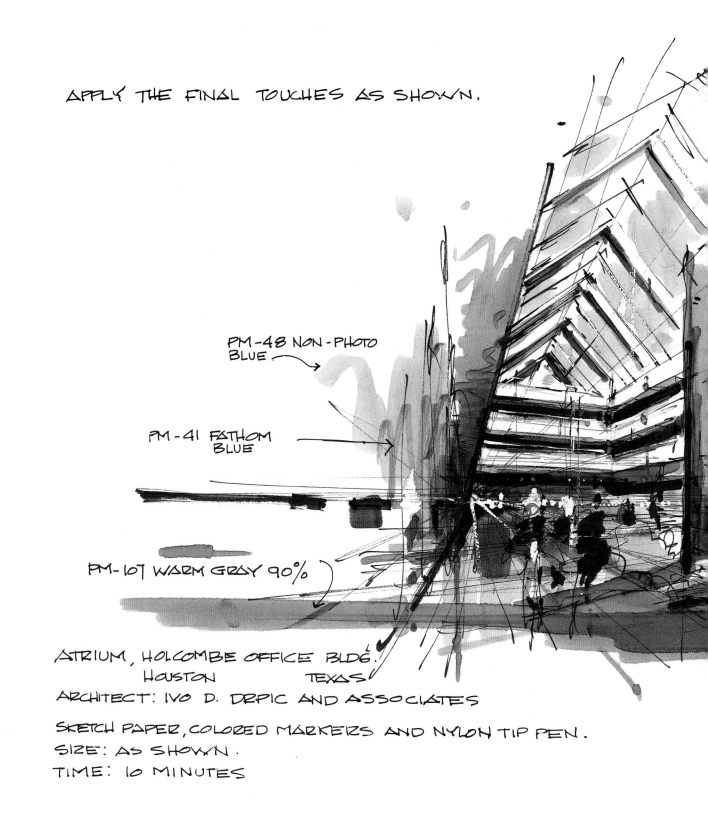

PM-48 NON-PHOTO
BLUE

PM-41 FATHOM
BLUE

PM-107 WARM GRAY 90%

ATRIUM, HOLCOMBE OFFICE BLDG.
HOUSTON          TEXAS
ARCHITECT: IVO D. DRPIC AND ASSOCIATES

SKETCH PAPER, COLORED MARKERS AND NYLON TIP PEN.
SIZE: AS SHOWN.
TIME: 10 MINUTES

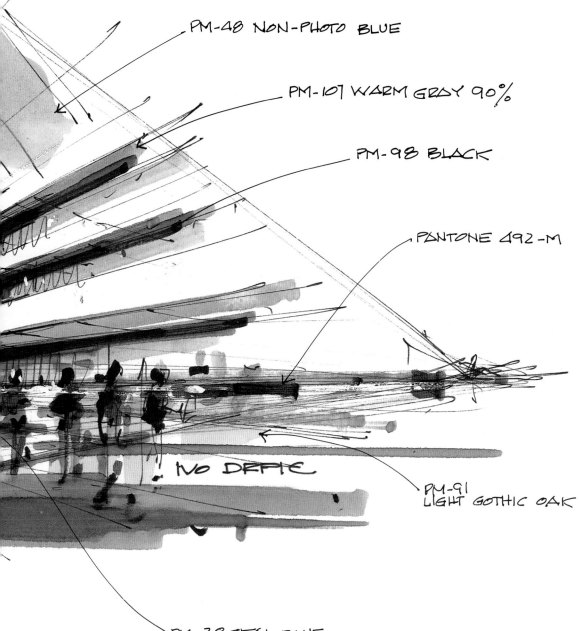

PM-48 NON-PHOTO BLUE

PM-107 WARM GRAY 90%

PM-98 BLACK

PANTONE 492-M

NO DRFIE

PM-91
LIGHT GOTHIC OAK

PM-38 TEAL BLUE

## COMPLEX SPACE IN ONE-POINT PERSPECTIVE

AFTER SELECTING A VIEW, START
SKETCHING AS SHOWN. IN THIS
TYPE OF SKETCH I WORK A
LITTLE MORE WITH THE LINES,
KEEPING THE SKETCH VERY LOOSE.

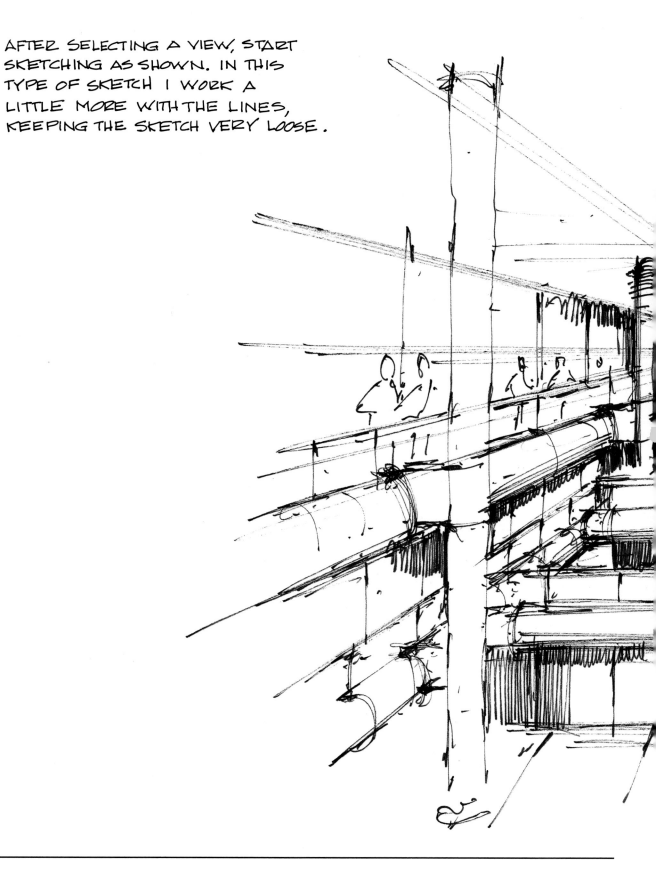

START ADDING THE COLORS
GRADUALLY, AS SHOWN.

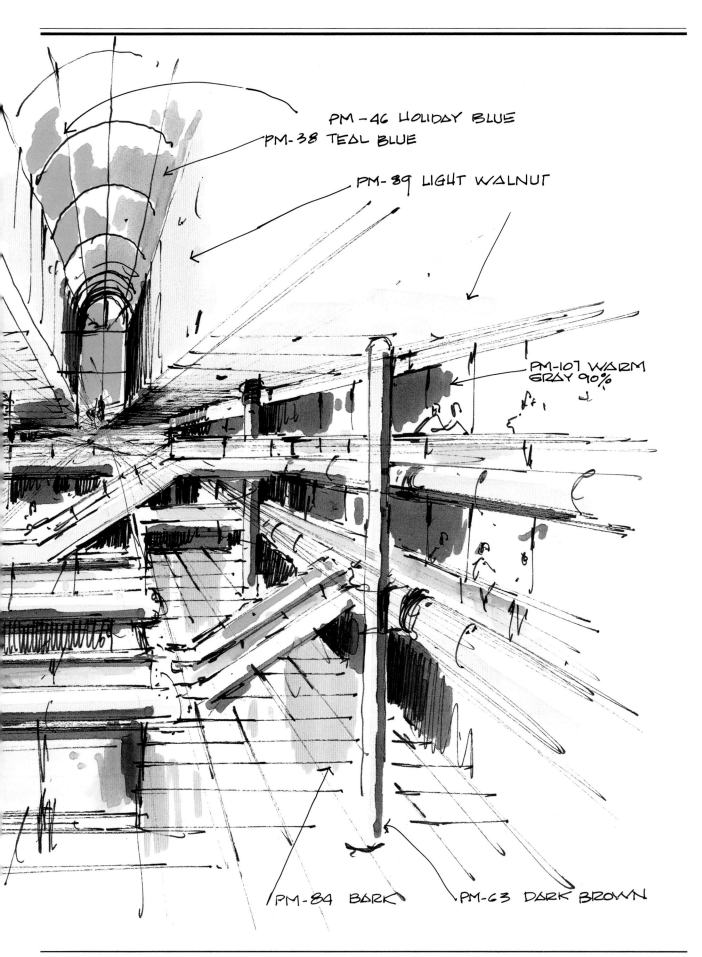

PM-46 HOLIDAY BLUE

PM-38 TEAL BLUE

PM-89 LIGHT WALNUT

PM-107 WARM GRAY 90%

PM-84 BARK        PM-63 DARK BROWN

ADD THE FINAL TOUCHES.

PM-89 LIGHT WALNUT

PM-98 BLACK

PM-59
LAVENDER

PM-46
HOLIDAY BLUE

NORTHWEST CENTER, HOUSTON, TEXAS
ARCHITECT: IVO D. DRPIC AND ASSOCIATES
SKETCH PAPER, COLORED MARKERS.
SIZE: AS SHOWN    TIME: 30 MINUTES

IVO DRPIC

PM-38 TEAL BLUE

PM-84 BARK

PM-89 LIGHT WALNUT

PM-5
SCARLET LAKE

PM-63 DARK BROWN

PM-69 YELLOW OCHRE

PM-98
BLACK

## COMPLEX SPACE IN TWO-POINT PERSPECTIVE

AGAIN, THE DIFFERENCE WITH THE PRECEDING
DEMONSTRATION IS THAT YOU WORK WITH
TWO VANISHING POINTS INSTEAD OF ONE.
HOWEVER, THE PROCEDURE IS THE SAME.

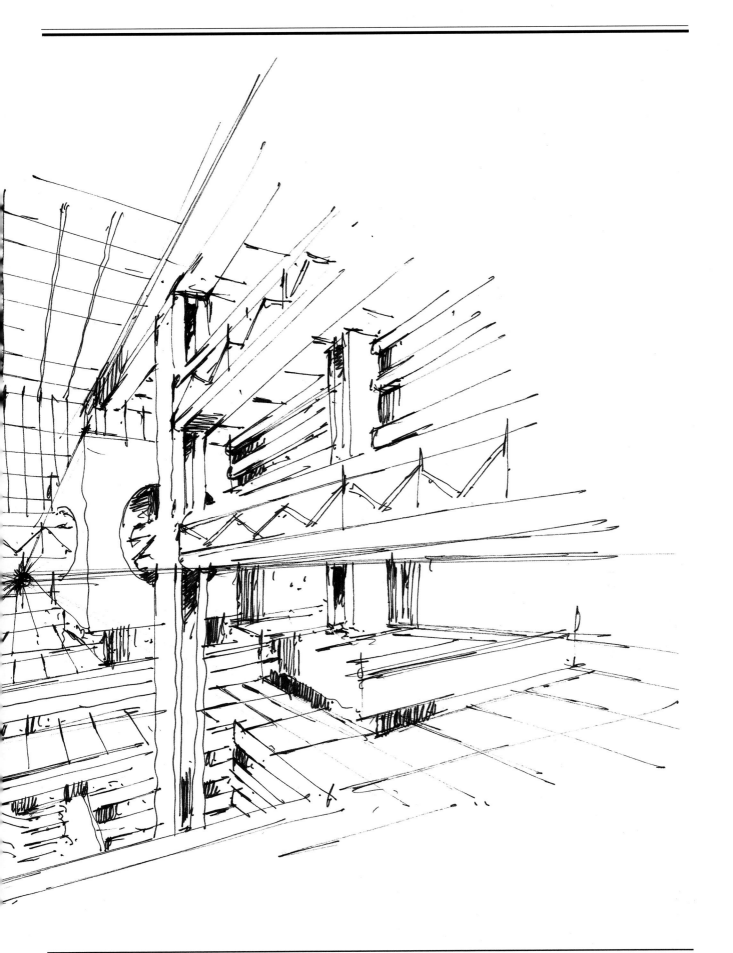

APPLY THE COLORS GRADUALLY AND
SLOWLY.

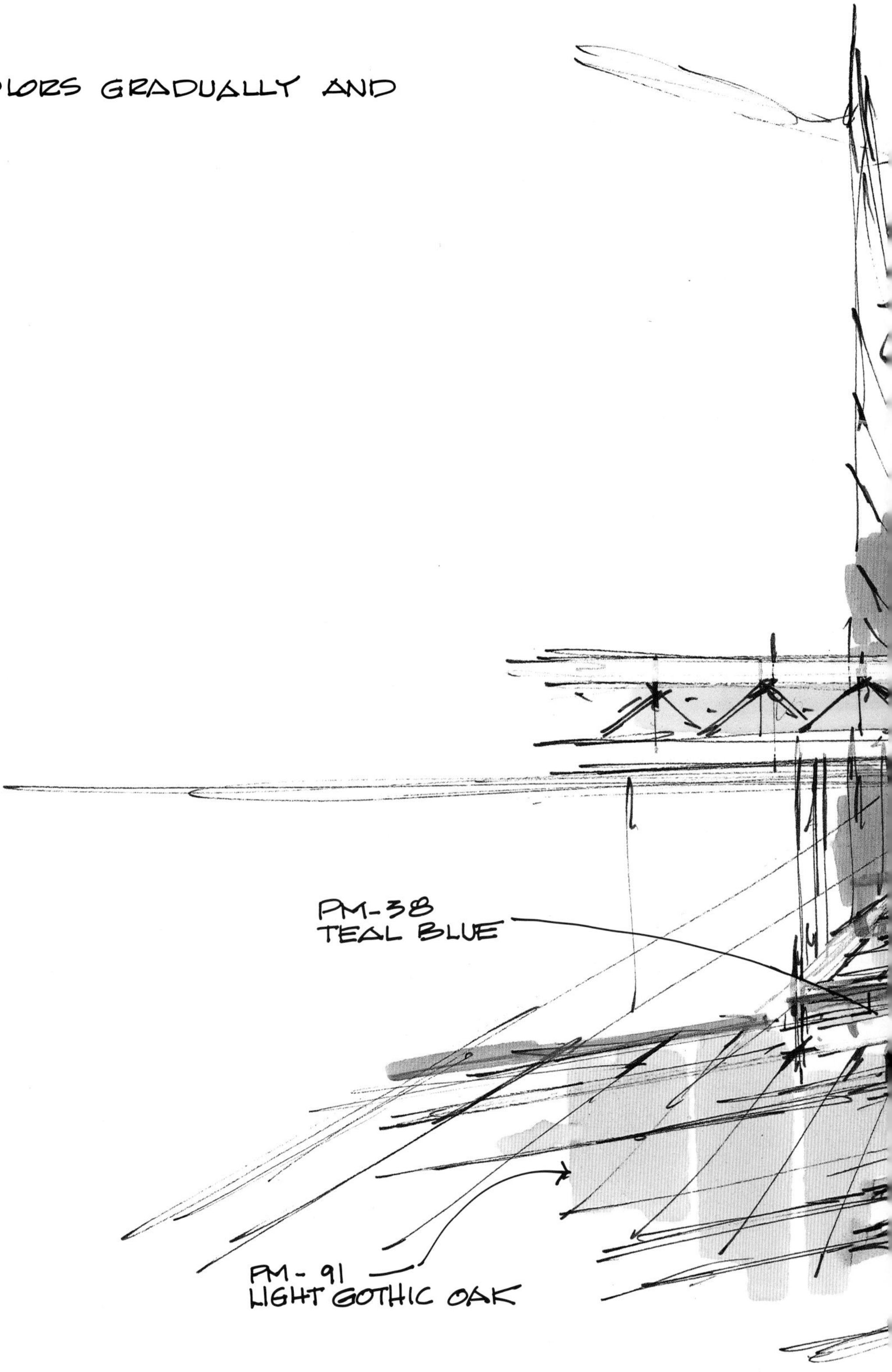

PM-38
TEAL BLUE

PM - 91
LIGHT GOTHIC OAK

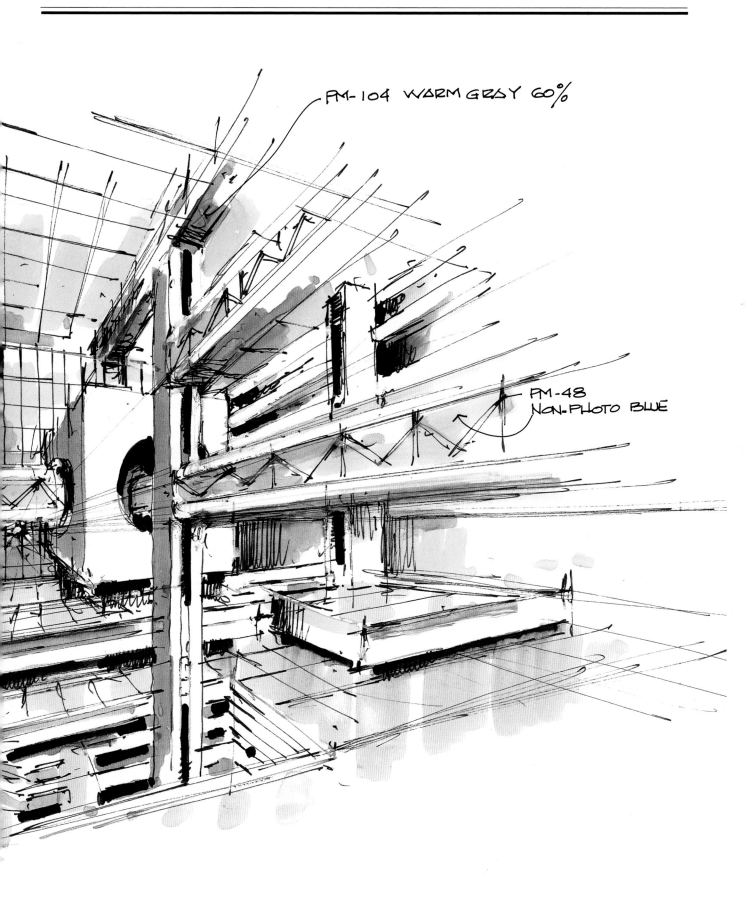

PM-104 WARM GRAY 60%

PM-48
NON-PHOTO BLUE

WORK THE FINAL DETAILS, AS SHOWN.

PM-104-WARM GRAY 60%

PM-107 WARM GRAY 90%

LOBBY (PRELIMINARY STUDY)
TEXTRONIC CENTER, HOUSTON, TEXAS
ARCHITECT: IVO D. DRPIC AND ASSOCIATES

SKETCH PAPER AND COLORED MARKERS
SIZE: AS SHOWN     TIME: 1 HOUR

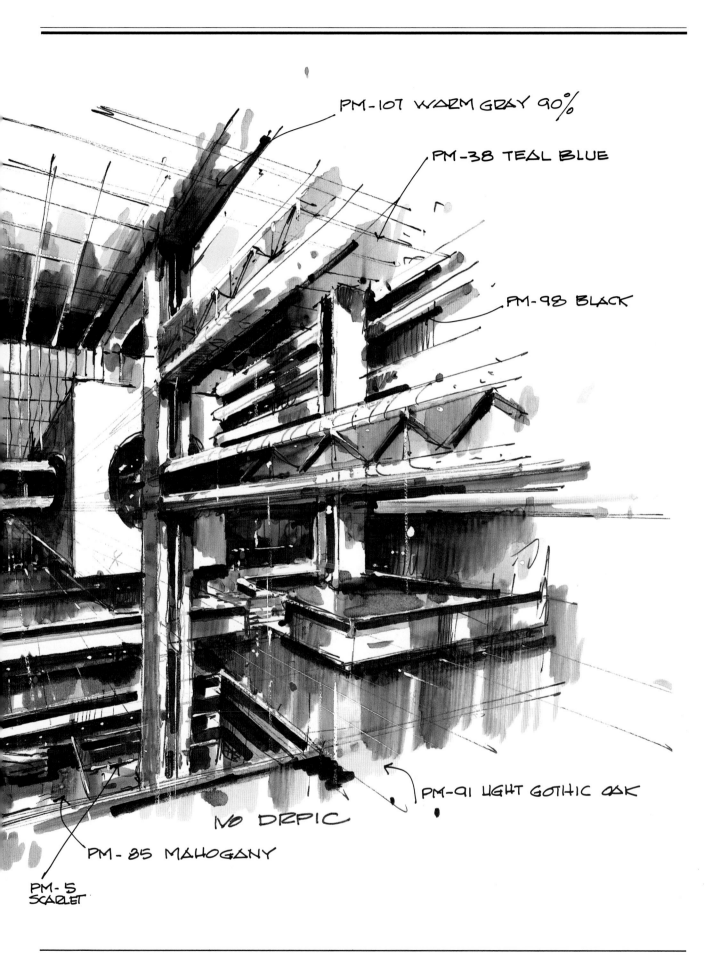

PM-107 WARM GRAY 90%

PM-38 TEAL BLUE

PM-98 BLACK

PM-91 LIGHT GOTHIC OAK

NO DRPIC

PM-85 MAHOGANY

PM-5 SCARLET

## SIMPLE SPACE IN AXONOMETRIC VIEW

AFTER DECIDING FROM WHICH POSITION
YOU WANT TO SEE THE SPACE, SKETCH
THE FLOOR PLAN, MAINTAINING THE
OPPOSITE SIDES (ELEVATIONS) OF THE
ROOM PARALLEL, AS SHOWN. ALSO LOCATE
THE FURNITURE IN THE SAME FASHION.

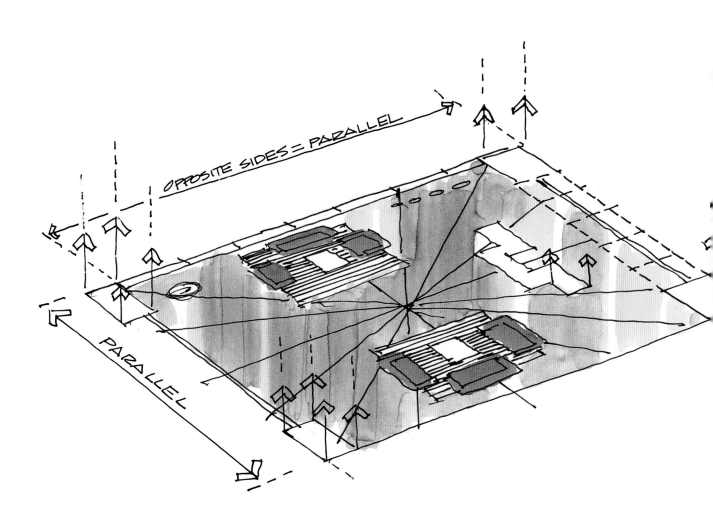

THE NEXT STEP WILL BE TO DRAW
PARALLEL VERTICAL LINES AS SHOWN.
(THE HEIGHT WILL BE IN THE SAME
SCALE WITH WHICH THE FLOOR PLAN
WAS DRAWN.)

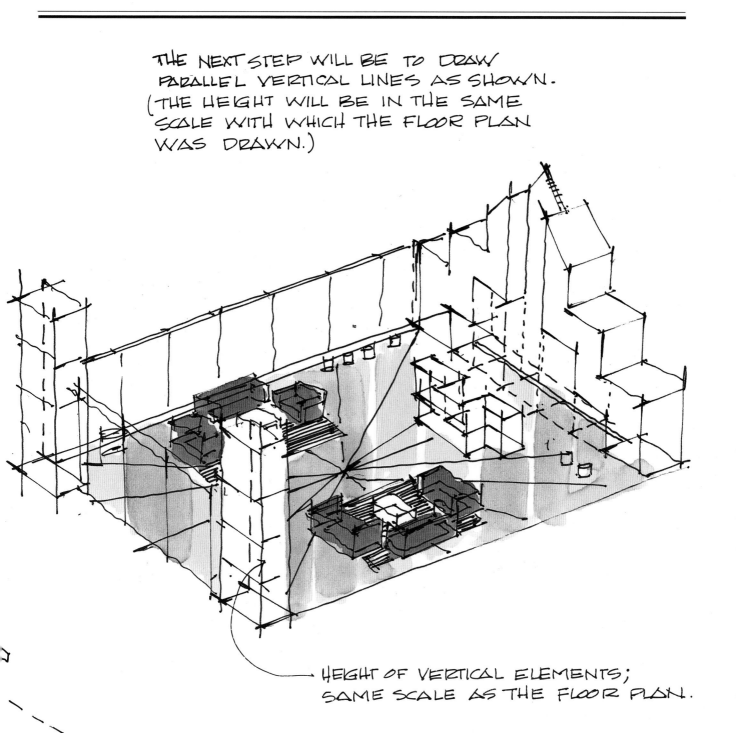

HEIGHT OF VERTICAL ELEMENTS;
SAME SCALE AS THE FLOOR PLAN.

KEEP APPLYNG COLORS, AS SHOWN.

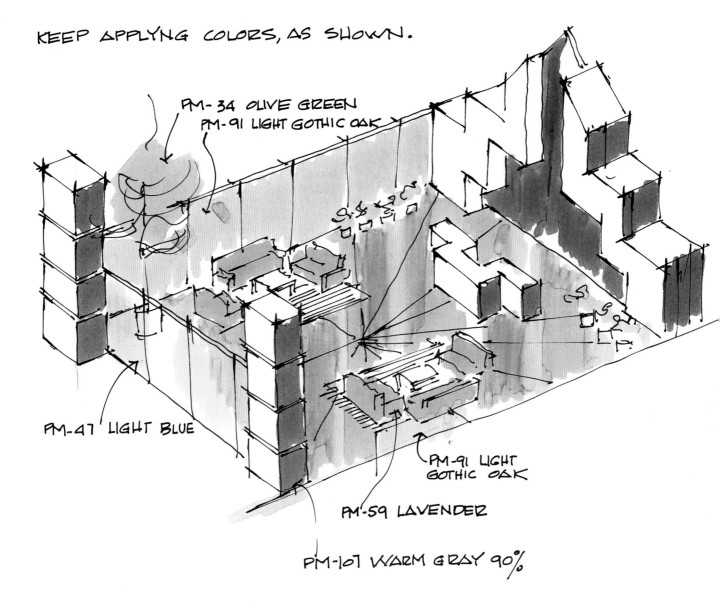

PM-34 OLIVE GREEN
PM-91 LIGHT GOTHIC OAK

PM-47 LIGHT BLUE

PM-91 LIGHT GOTHIC OAK

PM-59 LAVENDER

PM-107 WARM GRAY 90%

RECEPTION, OFFICE BLDG. HOUSTON, TEXAS
ARCHITECT: IVO D. DRPIC AND ASSOCIATES

SKETCH PAPER AND COLORED MARKERS
SIZE: AS SHOWN    TIME: 20 MINUTES EACH

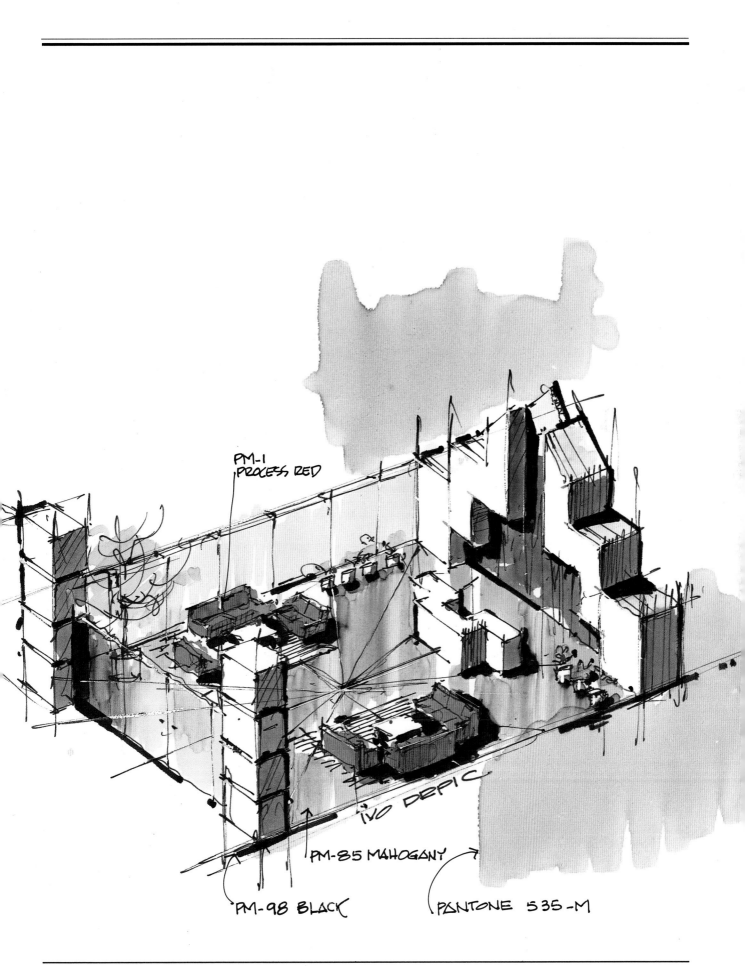

PM-1
PROCESS RED

PM-85 MAHOGANY

PM-98 BLACK

PANTONE 535-M

## COMPLEX SPACE IN AXONOMETRIC VIEW

THE PROCEDURE IS BASICALLY THE SAME
AS IN SIMPLE AXONOMETRIC SPACES, BUT
INSTEAD OF WORKING WITH ONE ROOM OR
SPACE, YOU WORK WITH SEVERAL.

PROCEDURE:
START FROM THE FLOOR PLAN
(MARKED WITH BLACK) AND BEGIN
PROJECTING PARALLEL LINES,
AS SHOWN IN ALL THE
INTERSECTIONS.(WALLS,
FURNITURE, AND SO ON).

APPLY COLORS VERY
CAREFULLY. BUT DO NOT
OVERWORK.

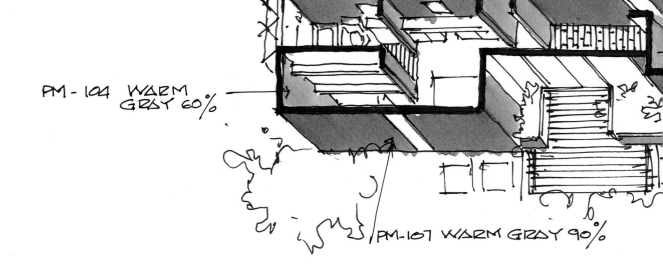

PM-98 BLACK ⟶

PM-104 WARM
GRAY 60%

PM-107 WARM GRAY 90%

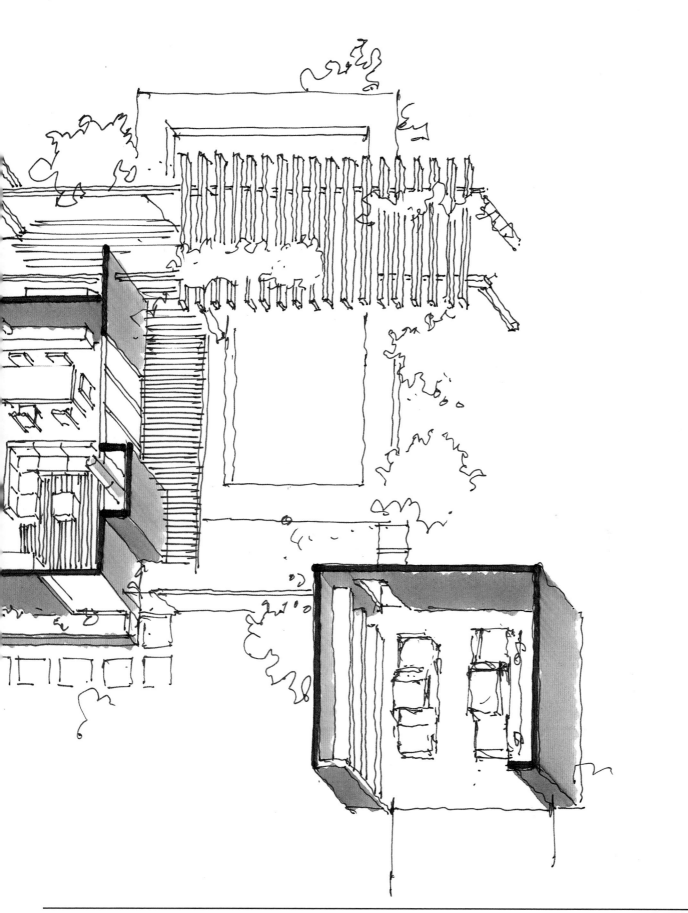

KEEP WORKING WITH THE COLORS,
AS SHOWN.

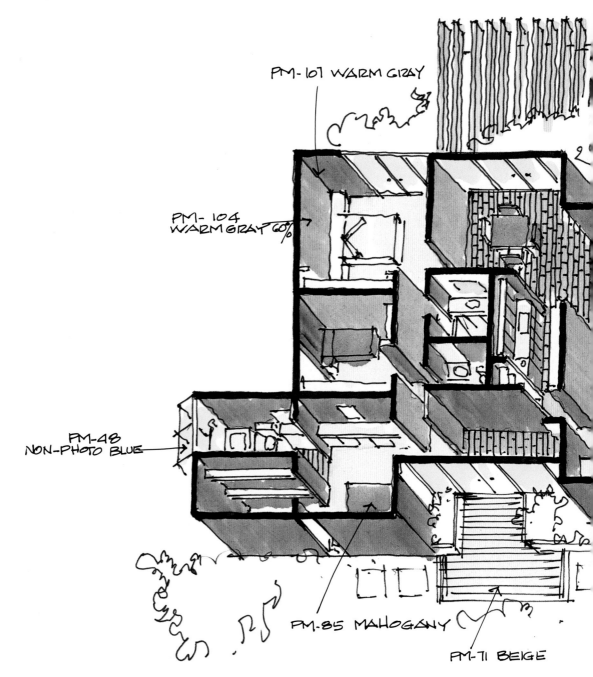

PM-107 WARM GRAY

PM- 104
WARM GRAY 60%

PM-48
NON-PHOTO BLUE

PM-85 MAHOGANY

PM-71 BEIGE

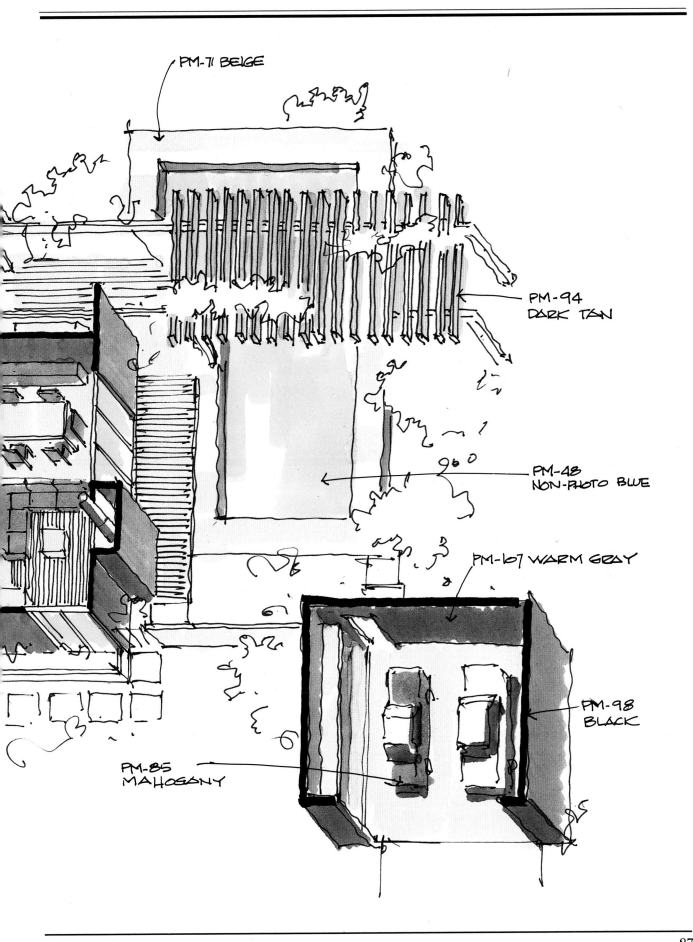

PM-71 BEIGE

PM-94
DARK TAN

PM-48
NON-PHOTO BLUE

PM-107 WARM GRAY

PM-98
BLACK

PM-85
MAHOGANY

APPLY THE FINAL TOUCHES, AS SHOWN.

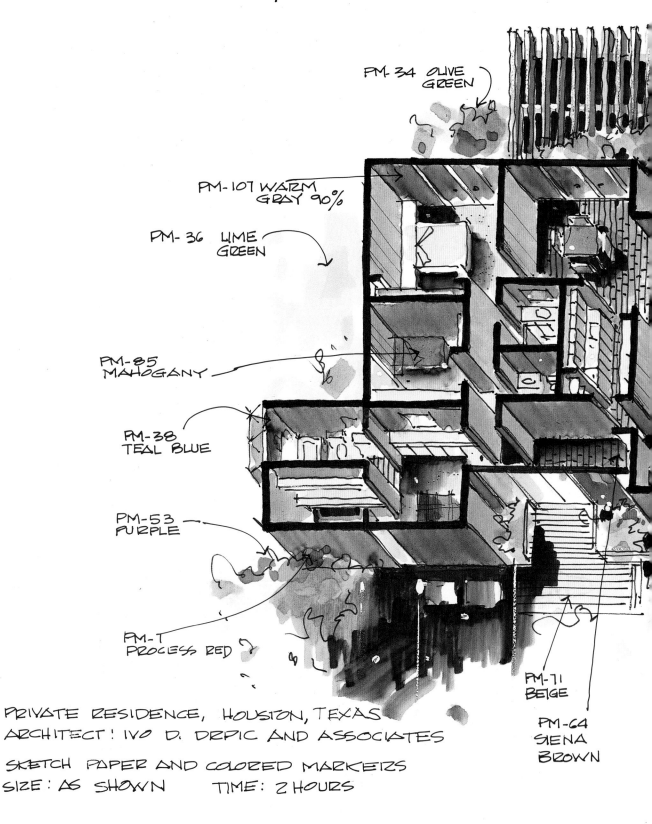

PM-34 OLIVE GREEN

PM-107 WARM GRAY 90%

PM-36 LIME GREEN

PM-85 MAHOGANY

PM-38 TEAL BLUE

PM-53 PURPLE

PM-T PROCESS RED

PM-71 BEIGE

PM-64 SIENA BROWN

PRIVATE RESIDENCE, HOUSTON, TEXAS
ARCHITECT: IVO D. DRPIC AND ASSOCIATES

SKETCH PAPER AND COLORED MARKERS
SIZE: AS SHOWN          TIME: 2 HOURS

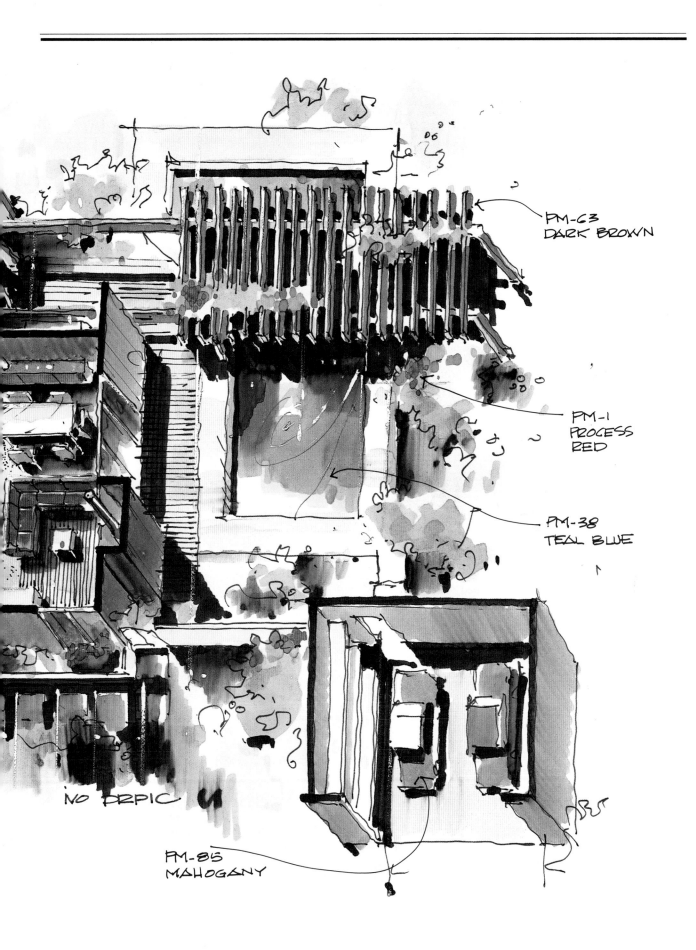

PM-63
DARK BROWN

PM-1
PROCESS
RED

PM-38
TEAL BLUE

NO DRPIC

PM-85
MAHOGANY

# SHADOWS CAST BY ARTIFICIAL LIGHT

THE DIFFERENCE BETWEEN NATURAL
AND ARTIFICIAL LIGHT IS THAT NATURAL
LIGHT EMITS PARALLEL RAYS, WHILE
ARTIFICIAL LIGHT CREATES RAYS THAT
RADIATE FROM THE SOURCE.

WHEN SKETCHING ARTIFICIAL LIGHT, THE
VANISHING POINTS OF THE SHADOWS ARE
LOCATED DIRECTLY UNDER THE LIGHT
SOURCE; SOMETIMES, THE LOCATION IS
HARD TO FIND.

IN ORDER TO LOCATE SHADOW AREAS,
YOU MUST PROJECT LINES FROM THE
LIGHT SOURCE TO INTERSECT WITH THE
FREESTANDING OBJECTS IN THE SPACE
AND BEYOND TO THE FLOORS OR WALLS.
THE SHADOWS WILL THEN BE ACCURATE.

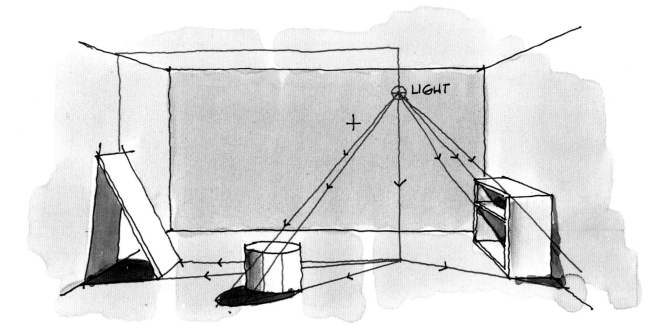

# SHADOWS CAST BY DAYLIGHT

BECAUSE THE SUN IS SUCH A GREAT DISTANCE AWAY, WE MAY CONSIDER THE INDIVIDUAL LIGHT RAYS TO BE PARALLEL. THUS THEY OBEY THE RULES OF PERSPECTIVE BY MEETING AT SOME COMMON VANISHING POINT.

DRAW A VERTICAL LINE FROM THE SUN'S LOCATION TO THE HORIZON, AND PROJECT LINES THROUGH THE SOURCE OF DAYLIGHT, AS SHOWN. THIS PROCEDURE WILL GIVE A GENERAL IDEA OF BOTH LIGHT AND SHADOW AREAS.

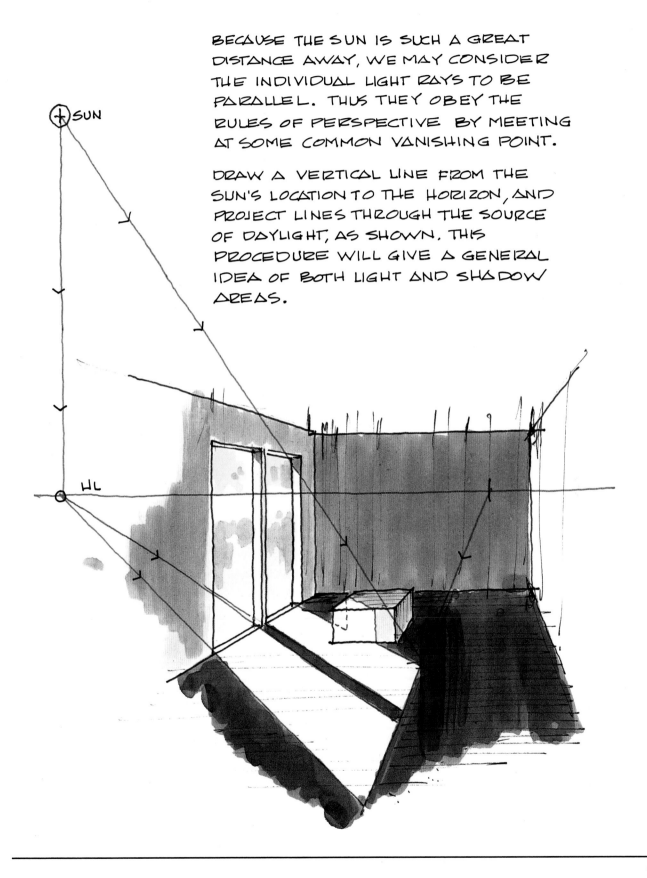

# SURFACES, ENTOURAGE, AND ATMOSPHERIC EMPHASIS

THE NEXT TWELVE DEMONSTRATIONS CONCENTRATE ON THREE KINDS OF PROBLEMS COMMON IN INTERIOR SKETCHING.

THE FIRST FOUR SHOW HOW TO SIMULATE SPECIFIC SURFACES: GLASS, WOOD, WATER, AND METAL AND OTHER HARD REFLECTIVE SURFACES.

THE NEXT FOUR ARE COMMON ELEMENTS OF ENTOURAGE: A CHAIR, A GROUP OF CHAIRS, PEOPLE, AND PLANTS.

THE FINAL FOUR SHOW HOW TO MANIPULATE A SKETCH TO PRODUCE RENDERINGS WITH SPECIFIC ATMOSPHERIC EFFECTS. I HAVE SELECTED A HIGH-TECH LOOK, A SPACE SEEN AT NIGHT, AN OPULENT EFFECT, AND A RENDERING THAT EMPHASIZES A FEELING OF COMFORT.

IVO DRPIC

# GLASS AND MARBLE SURFACES

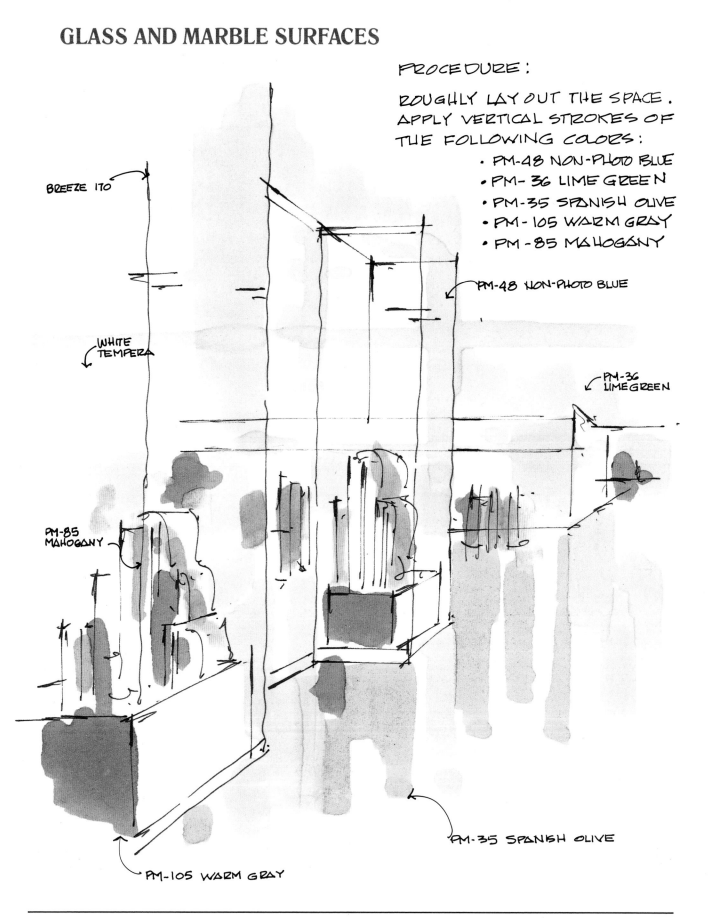

PROCEDURE:

ROUGHLY LAY OUT THE SPACE.
APPLY VERTICAL STROKES OF
THE FOLLOWING COLORS:
- PM-48 NON-PHOTO BLUE
- PM-36 LIME GREEN
- PM-35 SPANISH OLIVE
- PM-105 WARM GRAY
- PM-85 MAHOGANY

PM-48 NON-PHOTO BLUE

PM-36 LIME GREEN

BREEZE 170

WHITE TEMPERA

PM-85 MAHOGANY

PM-35 SPANISH OLIVE

PM-105 WARM GRAY

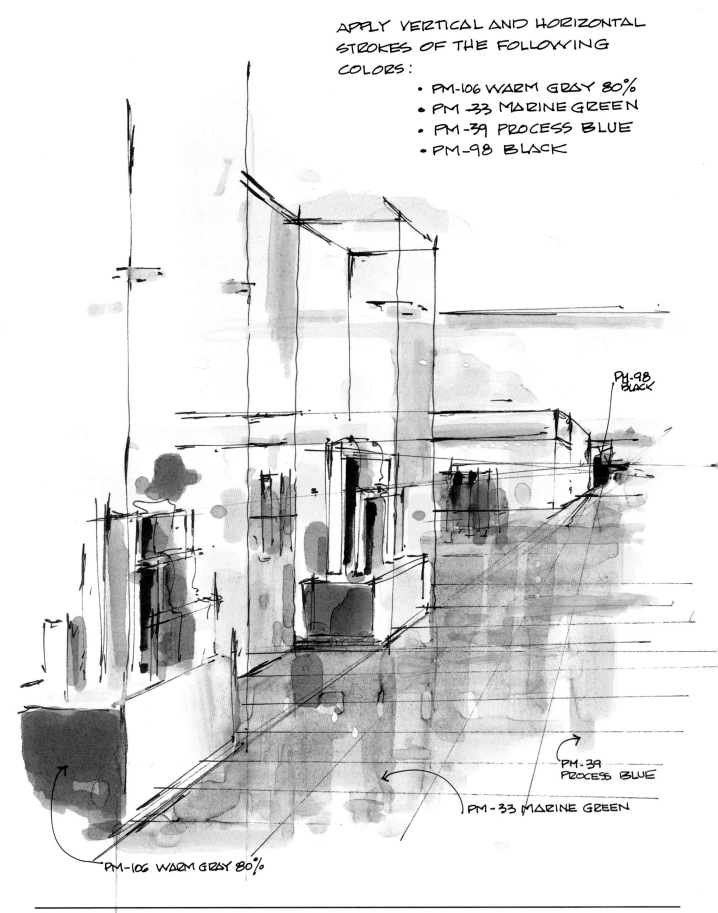

APPLY VERTICAL AND HORIZONTAL STROKES OF THE FOLLOWING COLORS:

- PM-106 WARM GRAY 80%
- PM-33 MARINE GREEN
- PM-39 PROCESS BLUE
- PM-98 BLACK

PM-98 BLACK

PM-39 PROCESS BLUE

PM-33 MARINE GREEN

PM-106 WARM GRAY 80%

PM-33 MARINE GREEN

TOUCH-UP:

DEFINE THE WEAK AREAS
WITH PM-98 BLACK, AS
SHOWN.
REAPPLY PM-35 SPANISH
OLIVE USING VERTICAL STROKES.
APPLY PM-33 MARINE GREEN,
AS SHOWN.

ADD TOUCHES OF WHITE,
RED, AND ORANGE
TEMPERA, BUT
DO NOT
OVERWORK.

IVO DRPIC

# WOOD SURFACES AND FINISHES

PROCEDURE:

ROUGHLY LAY OUT THE SPACE.
APPLY VERTICAL STROKES OF THE FOLLOWING COLORS:

- PM-89 LIGHT WALNUT
- PM-62 SEPIA
- PM-77 DARK BRICK RED
- PM-83 CEDAR
- PM-103 WARM GRAY 50%

PM-89 LIGHT WALNUT

PM-77 DARK BRICK RED

PM-103 WARM GRAY 50%

PM-77 DARK BRICK RED

PM-62 SEPIA

PM-83 CEDAR

CONTINUE TO ADD THE FOLLOWING COLORS, AS SHOWN.

- PM-84 BARK
- PM-98 BLACK
- PM-77 DARK BRICK RED
- PM-35 SPANISH OLIVE
- PM-34 OLIVE GREEN
- PM-107 WARM GRAY 90%

THE SKETCH IS NOW READY FOR THE FINAL TOUCHES.

INTERMIX THE WOOD COLORS, AS SHOWN (USING
PM-89 LIGHT WALNUT).
REINFORCE THE SKETCH WITH PM-98 BLACK, AS SHOWN.
ADD WOOD GRAIN LINES WITH BREEZE 170 PEN,
AS SHOWN.
ADD TOUCHES OF WHITE AND RED TEMPERA.
ADD A FEW TOUCHES OF (PM-47) LIGHT BLUE.
ADD HORIZONTAL PEN STROKES WITH BREEZE 170
PEN TO THE CARPET, AS SHOWN.
TOUCH UP THE SKETCH WITH A SHARPIE PEN.

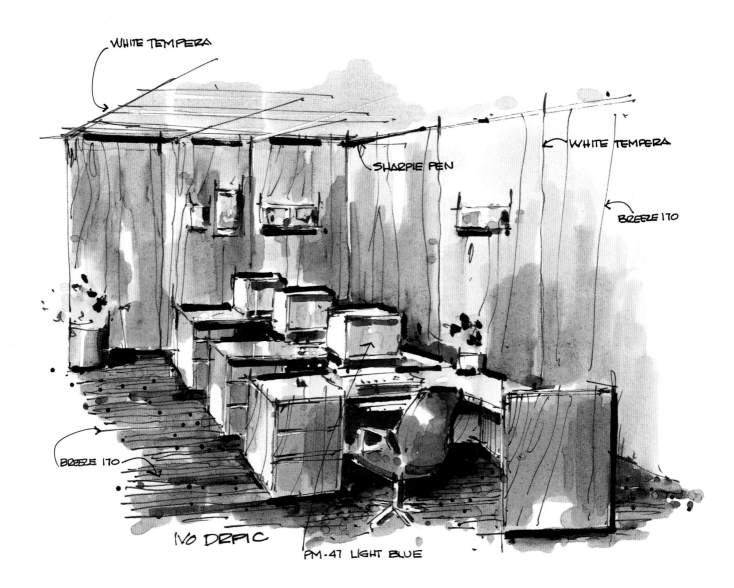

# WATER

PROCEDURE:
ROUGHLY LAY OUT THE SPACE.
APPLY VERTICAL STROKES OF THE FOLLOWING COLORS:

- PM-48 NON-PHOTO BLUE
- PM-47 LIGHT BLUE
- PM-103 WARM GRAY 50%
- PM-107 WARM GRAY 90%

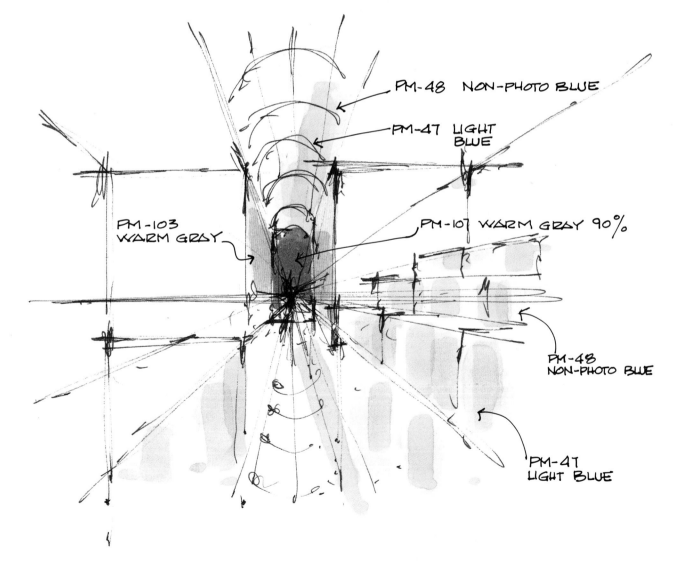

CONTINUE TO ADD THE FOLLOWING COLORS:

- PM-37 AQUAMARINE
- PM-107 WARM GRAY 90%
- PM-103 WARM GRAY 50%

THE SKETCH IS NOW READY FOR THE FINAL TOUCHES.

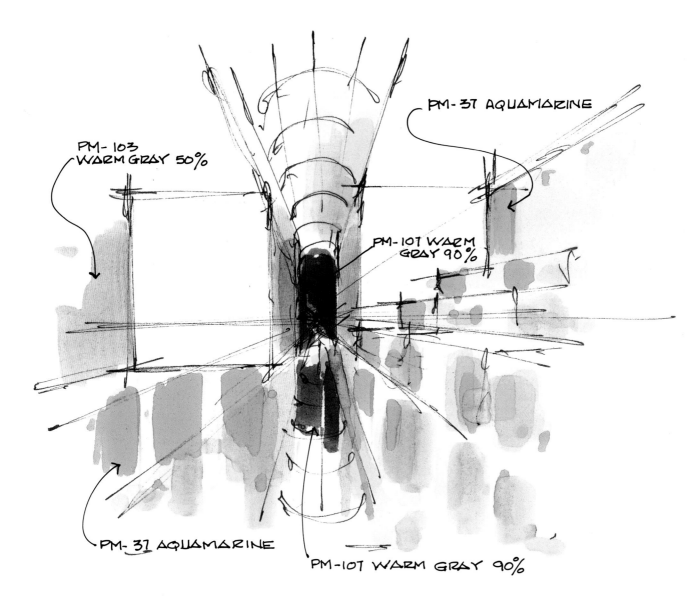

ADD (PM-98) BLACK, AS SHOWN.
ADD HORIZONTAL STROKES OF (PM-37) AQUAMARINE.
ADD VERTICAL REFLECTIONS WITH WHITE, RED, AND
ORANGE TEMPERA.
ADD VERTICAL AND WAVY LINES WITH BREEZE
170 (BLACK PEN).

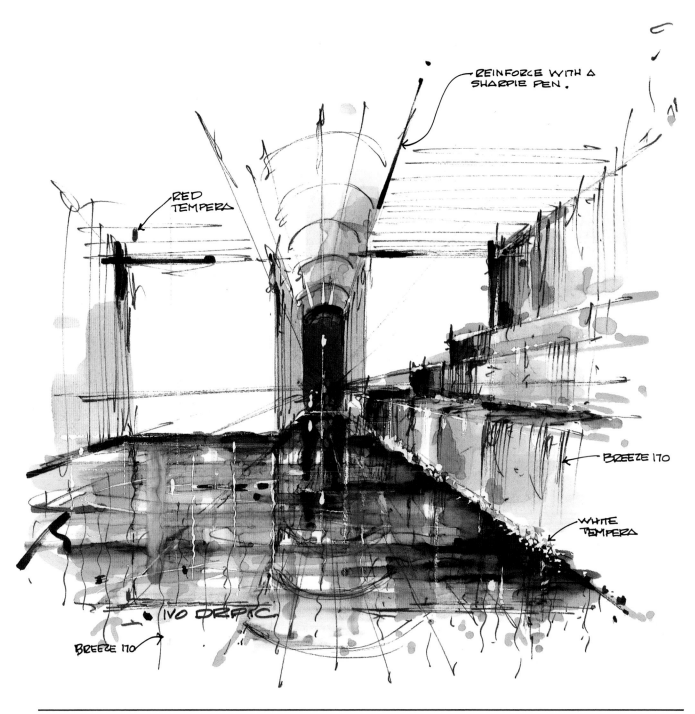

REINFORCE WITH A
SHARPIE PEN.

RED
TEMPERA

BREEZE 170

WHITE
TEMPERA

IVO DRPTC

BREEZE 170

# METAL AND OTHER HARD REFLECTIVE SURFACES

PROCEDURE:

ROUGHLY LAY OUT THE SKETCH.
APPLY VERTICAL STROKES OF THE FOLLOWING COLORS:

- WHITE MARKER (PENTEL)
- PM-49 BLUE VIOLET
- PM-97 BLUE GRAY
- PM-111 COLD GRAY
- PM-98 BLACK

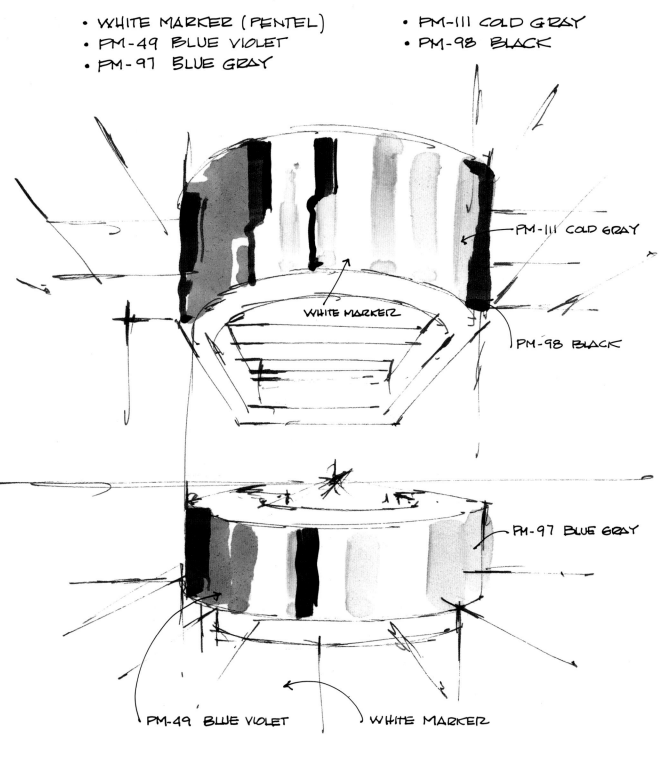

PM-111 COLD GRAY

WHITE MARKER

PM-98 BLACK

PM-97 BLUE GRAY

PM-49 BLUE VIOLET

WHITE MARKER

INTERMIX THE COLORS WITH VERTICAL STROKES. USE
PM-111 COLD GRAY MARKER.
REAPPLY PM-98 BLACK (AS SHOWN) TO REINFORCE
WEAK AREAS.
NOTE: MIX COLORS WHILE THEY ARE STILL WET. YOU
WILL HAVE TO WORK FAST.
APPLY VERTICAL STROKES TO THE CEILING, USING PM-111
COLD GRAY, AS SHOWN.

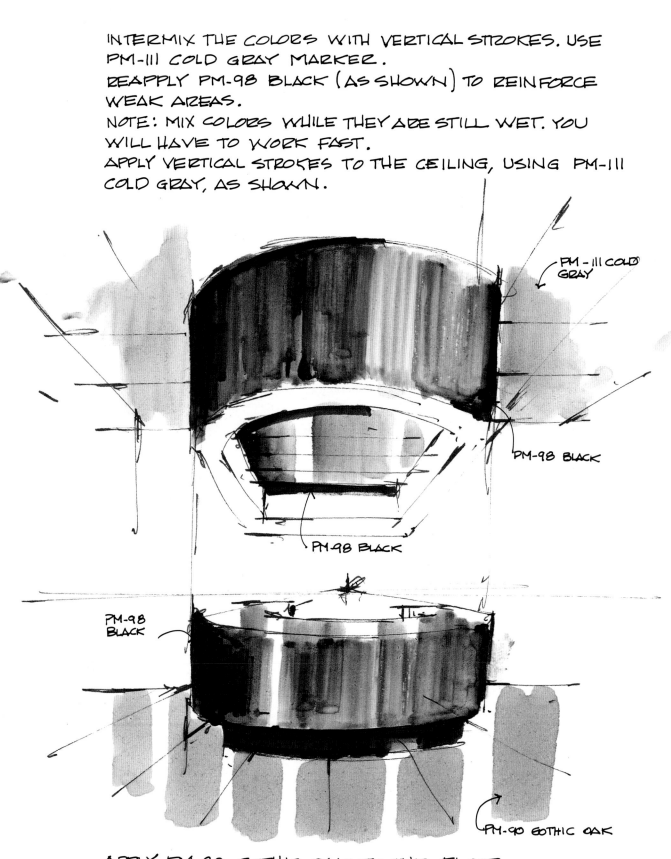

PM-111 COLD
GRAY

PM-98 BLACK

PM-98 BLACK

PM-98
BLACK

PM-90 GOTHIC OAK

APPLY PM-90 GOTHIC OAK TO THE FLOOR.

REAPPLY THE WHITE AND INTERMIX IT WITH THE OTHER COLORS IN VERTICAL STROKES.

APPLY VERTICAL STROKES OF PM-73 FLAGSTONE RED TO BACK WALL, AS SHOWN.

APPLY VERTICAL STROKES OF PM 77 DARK BRICK RED.

APPLY HORIZONTAL STROKES OF PM-73 FLAGSTONE RED TO THE FLOOR, AS SHOWN.

APPLY VERTICAL STROKES OF PM-111 COLD GRAY TO THE CEILING.

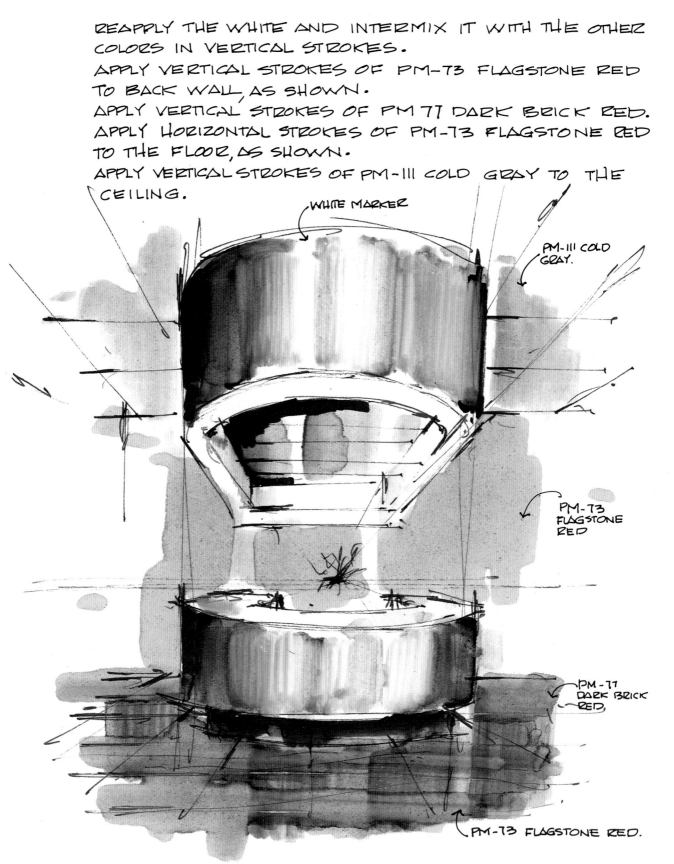

WHITE MARKER

PM-111 COLD GRAY.

PM-73 FLAGSTONE RED

PM-77 DARK BRICK RED.

PM-73 FLAGSTONE RED.

THE SKETCH IS NOW READY FOR A TOUCH UP.

TOUCH UP:

APPLY THE FOLLOWING COLORS:
PM-2 CHINESE RED (ABOVE THE DESK TOP)
PM-49 BLUE VIOLET (FLOOR AS SHOWN)
TOUCHES OF WHITE, RED, AND YELLOW TEMPERA

REINFORCE WEAK AREAS WITH PM-98 BLACK.

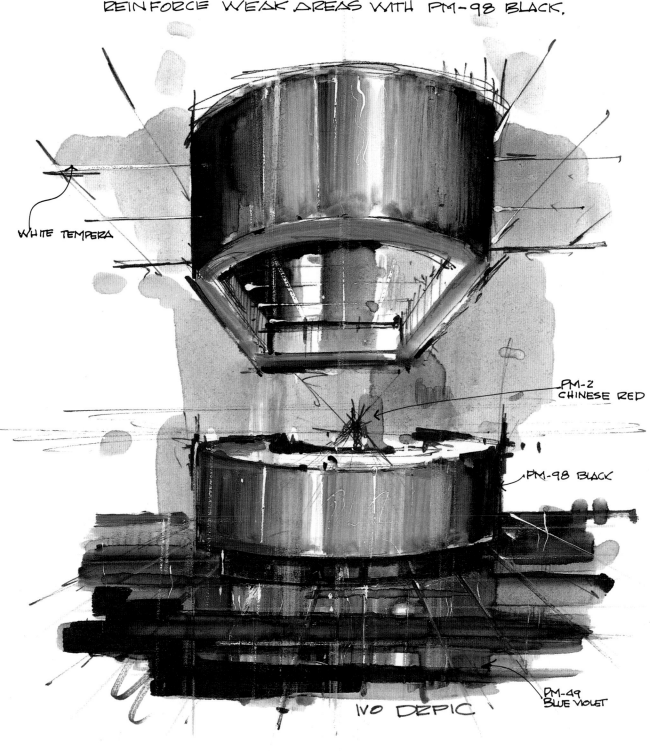

WHITE TEMPERA

PM-2
CHINESE RED

PM-98 BLACK

IVO DRPIC

PM-49
BLUE VIOLET

## CHAIR

THEN APPLY COLOR, AS SHOWN.

ROUGHLY SKETCH THE CHAIR.

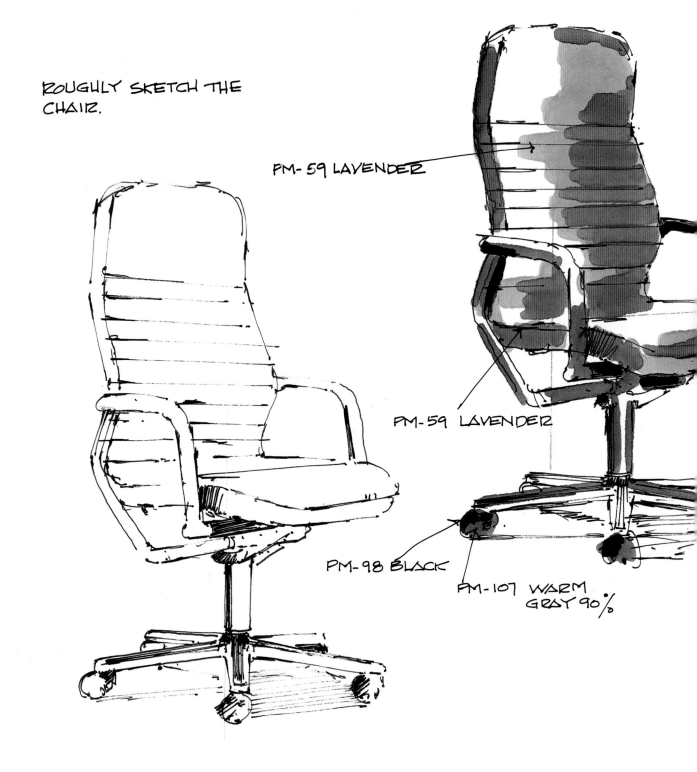

PM-59 LAVENDER

PM-59 LAVENDER

PM-98 BLACK

PM-107 WARM GRAY 90%

ADD FINAL TOUCHES.

PM-107-WARM GRAY 90%

PANTONE 549-M

PM-98 BLACK

PM-98 BLACK

IVO DRAC

ROUGHLY SKETCH THE
CHAIRS.

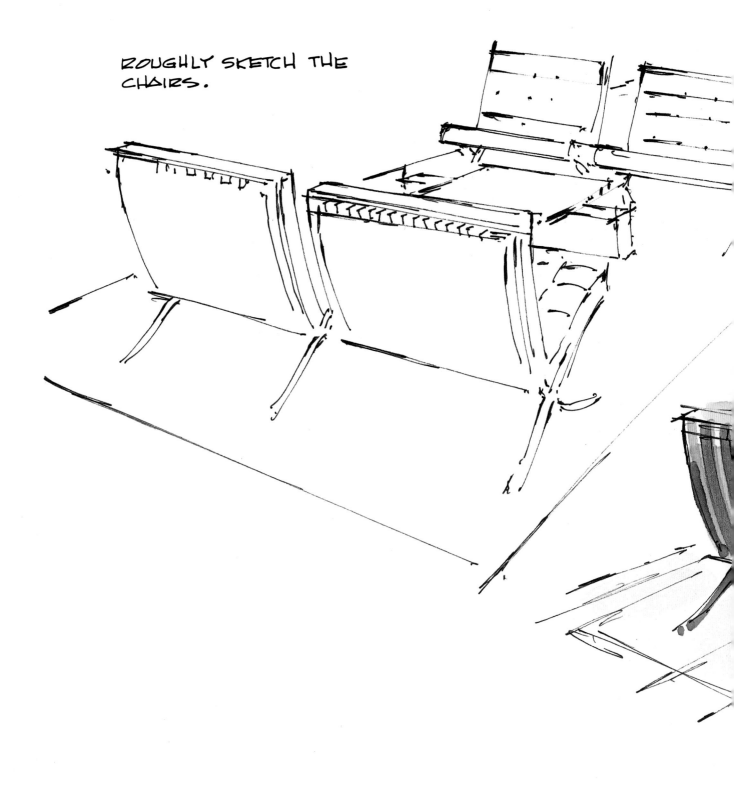

APPLY COLOR WITH FAST STROKES, AS SHOWN.
DO NOT WORRY IF COLOR GOES BEYOND
THE LIMITS OF THE SKETCH.

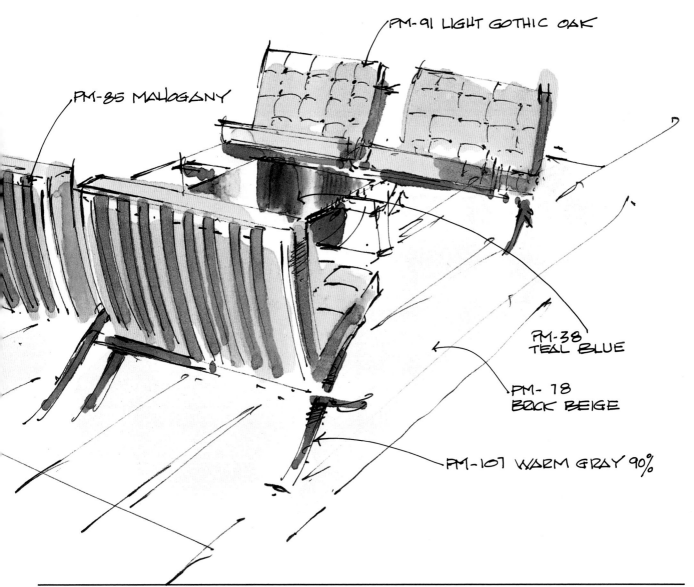

PM-91 LIGHT GOTHIC OAK

PM-85 MAHOGANY

PM-38
TEAL BLUE

PM-78
BRICK BEIGE

PM-107 WARM GRAY 90%

KEEP ADDING COLOR
GRADUALLY UNTIL
DESIRED RESULTS
ARE ACHIEVED.

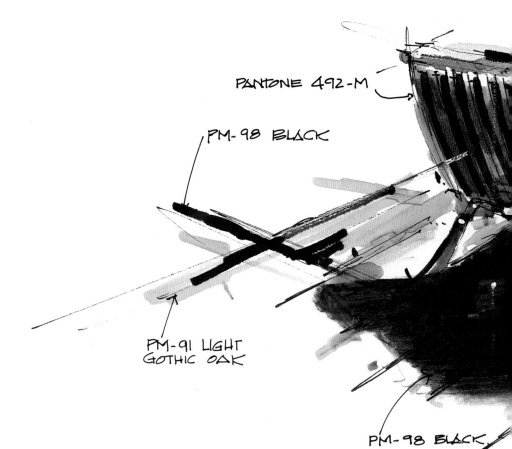

PANTONE 492-M

PM-98 BLACK

PM-91 LIGHT
GOTHIC OAK

PM-98 BLACK

PANTONE 535-M

PM-59
LAVENDER

IVO DRPIC

# PEOPLE

THERE ARE MANY WAYS TO SKETCH THE HUMAN FIGURE.
ONE OF THE EASIEST WAYS IS INDICATED BELOW.
KEEP THE FIGURES VERY SKETCHY AND ADD COLOR
AS SHOWN.

THE AMOUNT OF DETAIL IS DIRECTLY RELATED TO THE TYPE
OF DRAWING. FOR EXAMPLE, A ROUGH SKETCH SHOULD
HAVE ROUGH HUMAN FIGURES DRAWN.
A MORE FINISHED SKETCH HAS TO HAVE THE PEOPLE DRAWN
IN A SIMILARLY FINISHED MANNER.

NOTE: FOR MORE DETAILED AND COMPLETE DRAWINGS OF
THE HUMAN FIGURE, YOU CAN FIND SEVERAL EXCELLENT BOOKS
ON THE MARKET. I USE THEM VERY OFTEN. THEY ARE:
ENTOURAGE: A TRACING FILE, BY ERNEST BURDEN.
DRAWING FILE FOR ARCHITECTS, ILLUSTRATORS, BY MARC SZABO.

LOCATING AND SKETCHING
PEOPLE IN PERSPECTIVE
IS SIMPLE. JUST PROJECT
LINES AS SHOWN:

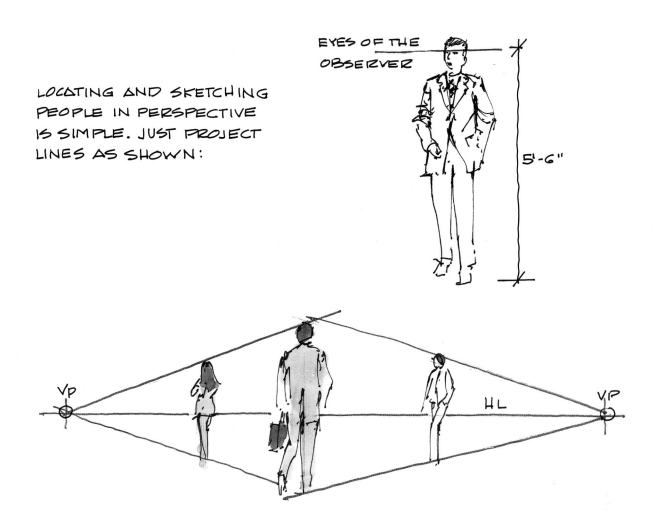

EYES OF THE
OBSERVER

5'-6"

VP                    HL                    VP

ANOTHER WAY TO LOCATE PEOPLE IN PERSPECTIVE
IS SHOWN BELOW.
THE HORIZON LINE PASSES THROUGH THE EYES OF THE
OBSERVER.

HORIZON

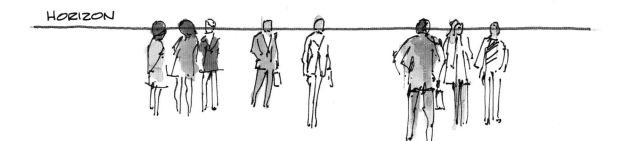

# PLANTS

WHEN SKETCHING INTERIOR SPACES, I KEEP THE
GREENERY ABSTRACT AND SIMPLE — UNLESS THE
SKETCH CALLS FOR A SPECIFIC PLANT OR GREAT
DETAIL. THE PLANTS SHOWN ON THESE TWO PAGES
SERVE MOST PURPOSES.

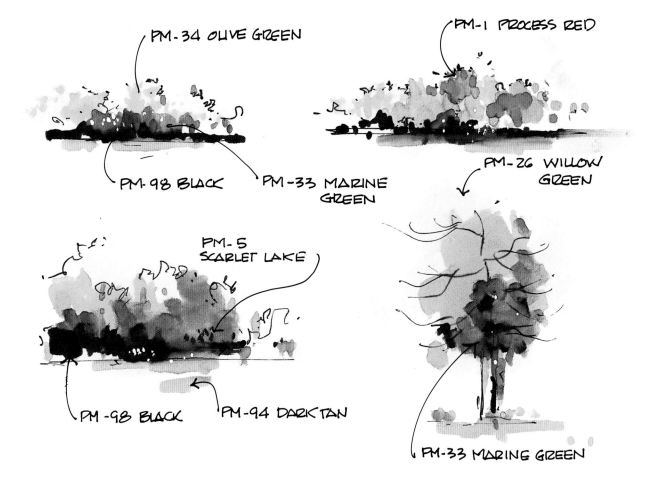

PM-34 OLIVE GREEN

PM-1 PROCESS RED

PM-26 WILLOW GREEN

PM-98 BLACK

PM-33 MARINE GREEN

PM-5 SCARLET LAKE

PM-98 BLACK

PM-94 DARK TAN

PM-33 MARINE GREEN

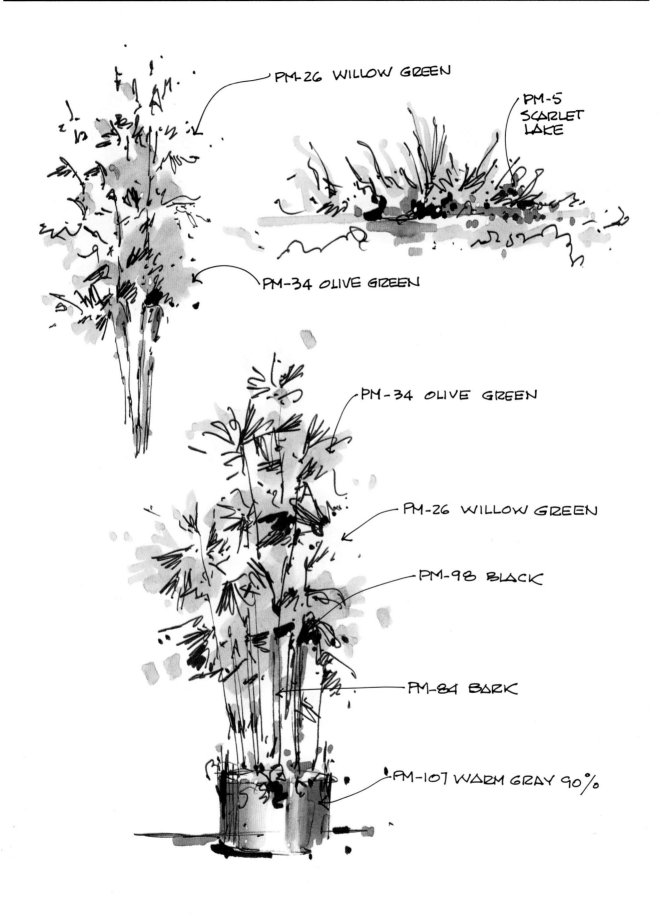

PM-26 WILLOW GREEN

PM-5 SCARLET LAKE

PM-34 OLIVE GREEN

PM-34 OLIVE GREEN

PM-26 WILLOW GREEN

PM-98 BLACK

PM-84 BARK

PM-107 WARM GRAY 90%

# ATMOSPHERIC EMPHASIS

AMONG OTHER THINGS, SKETCHES ARE SELLING TOOLS. WHEN A CLIENT IS LOOKING FOR A CERTAIN ATMOSPHERE, LOOK, OR MOOD, YOU CAN MAKE YOUR SKETCHES EVOKE THE "FEELING" OF THE SPACE — WHETHER HIGH TECH, COZY, SHOWY, OR SIMPLY COMFORTABLE.

## HIGH TECH

BOTH THE DYNAMIC POINT OF VIEW AND THE SUGGESTION OF SPACE-AGE SURFACING MATERIALS GIVE THIS COMPUTER ROOM AN ADVANCED, ALMOST FUTURISTIC LOOK.

DRAW THE SPACE QUITE ROUGHLY. THE EFFECTS OF SLEEKNESS AND BRIGHTNESS WILL BE ACHIEVED BY THE APPLICATION AND INTERMIXING OF COLOR.

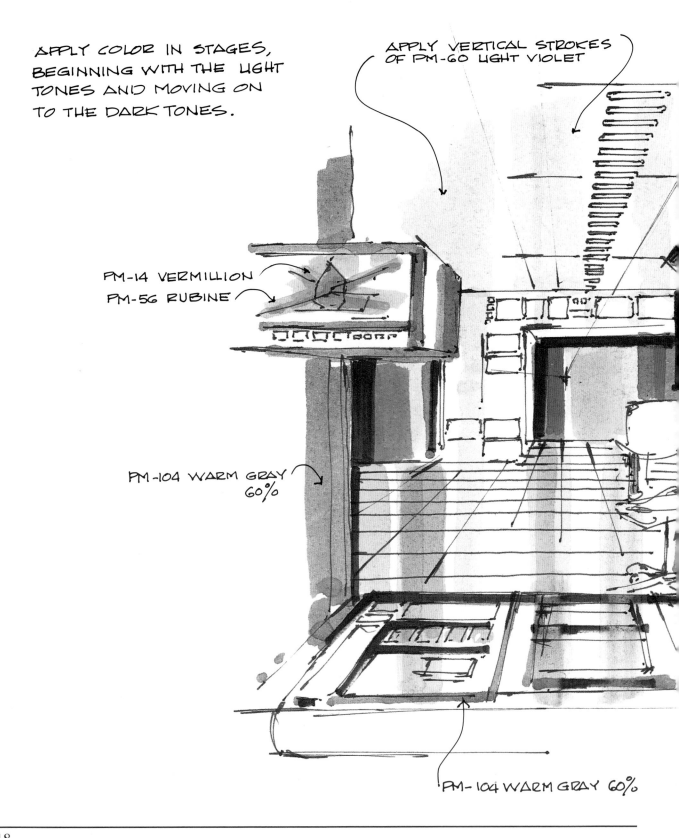

APPLY COLOR IN STAGES, BEGINNING WITH THE LIGHT TONES AND MOVING ON TO THE DARK TONES.

APPLY VERTICAL STROKES OF PM-60 LIGHT VIOLET

PM-14 VERMILLION
PM-56 RUBINE

PM-104 WARM GRAY 60%

PM-104 WARM GRAY 60%

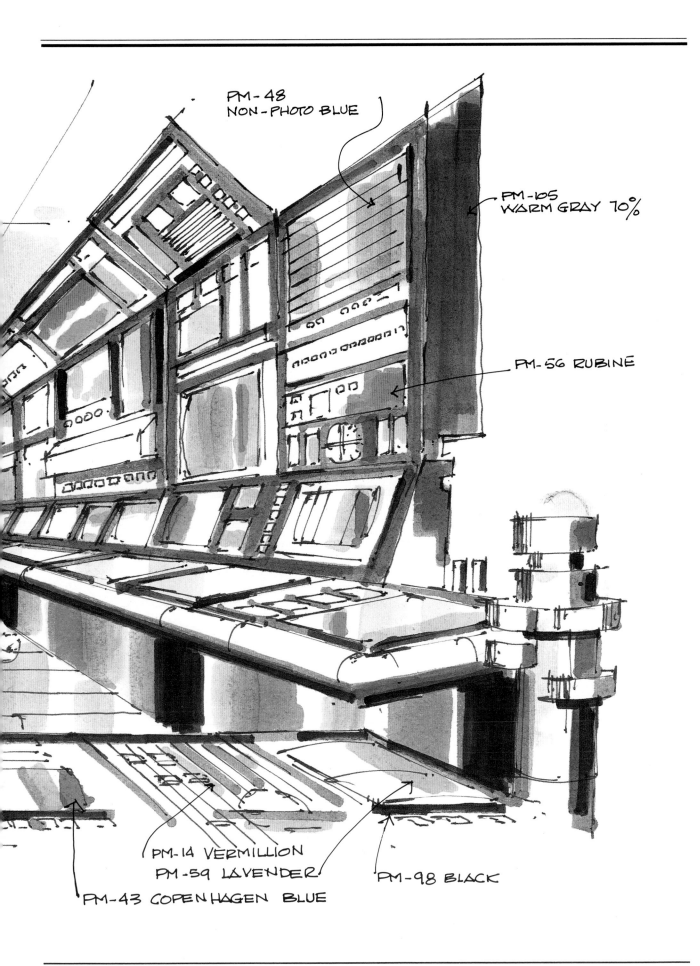

PM-48
NON-PHOTO BLUE

PM-105
WARM GRAY 70%

PM-56 RUBINE

PM-14 VERMILLION
PM-59 LAVENDER

PM-98 BLACK

PM-43 COPENHAGEN BLUE

INTERMIX THE COLORS, AS SHOWN, USING
THE FINE AND BROAD TIPS OF A SOFT
COLOR MARKER (IN THIS CASE PM-60
LIGHT VIOLET).

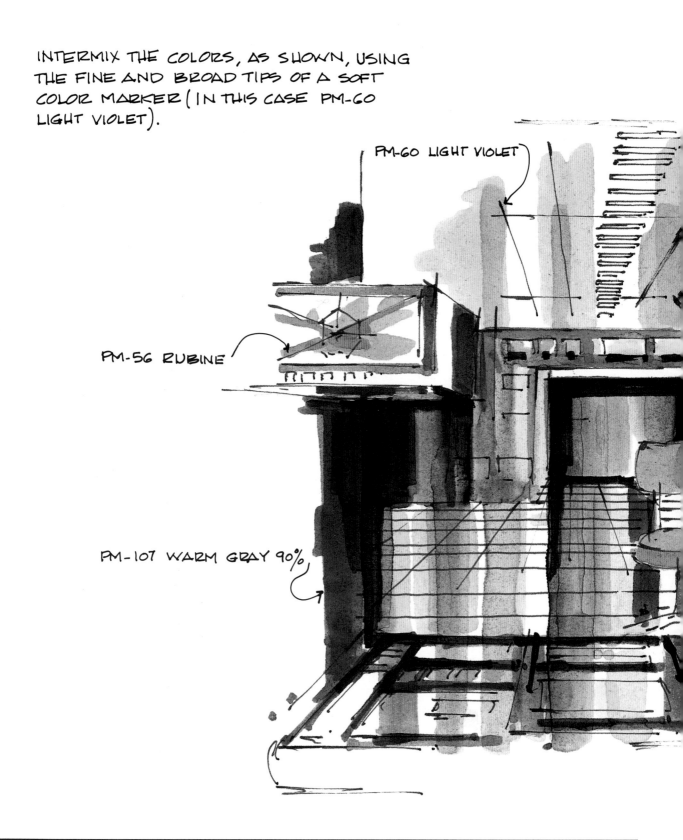

PM-60 LIGHT VIOLET

PM-56 RUBINE

PM-107 WARM GRAY 90%

PM-107
WARM GRAY

PM-98 BLACK

PM-98 BLACK

PM-43 COPENHAGEN BLUE

APPLY THE FINAL TOUCHES, AS SHOWN.
KEEP INTERMIXING THE COLORS UNTIL
YOU SOFTEN THE METALLIC AND GLASS
SURFACES
TOUCH UP WITH WHITE MARKER (PENTEL).

TIME: 1½ HOURS

COMPUTER ROOM
ARCHITECT: IVO D. DRPIC AND
            ASSOCIATES

IVO DRPIC

# NIGHT

SHOWING A SPACE AT NIGHT CAN SUGGEST ITS COZINESS;
IT CAN JUST AS WELL HEIGHTEN ITS GLAMOUR.

IN THIS SKETCH, SHOWING AN APARTMENT IN A HIGH-RISE
URBAN CONDOMINIUM, THE NIGHTIME SKYLINE SEEN
THROUGH THE FULL GLASS ELEVATION IS USED TO LEND A
CHIC, GLAMOUROUS ATMOSPHERE TO THE SPACE.

WHEN SKETCHING THIS LAY OUT, OR SPACE, KEEP IT
VERY BASIC. THE REST OF THE SKETCH IS GOING TO BE
MANIPULATED THROUGH THE USE OF COLOR.

APPLY THE COLORS AS SHOWN.

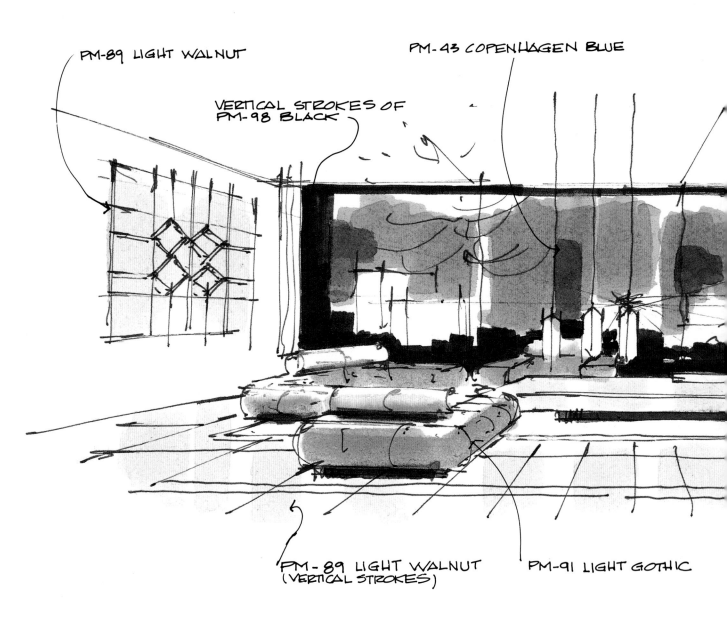

PM-89 LIGHT WALNUT

PM-43 COPENHAGEN BLUE

VERTICAL STROKES OF
PM-98 BLACK

PM-89 LIGHT WALNUT
(VERTICAL STROKES)

PM-91 LIGHT GOTHIC

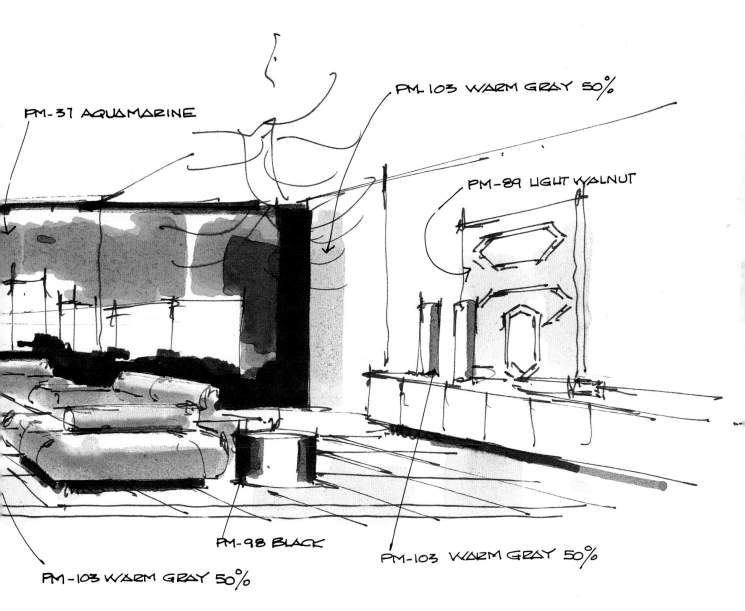

PM-37 AQUAMARINE

PM-103 WARM GRAY 50%

PM-89 LIGHT WALNUT

PM-98 BLACK

PM-103 WARM GRAY 50%

PM-103 WARM GRAY 50%

INTERMIX THE COLORS, AS SHOWN, USING THE FINE
AND BROAD TIPS OF A SOFT COLOR MARKER
(IN THIS CASE PM-47 LIGHT BLUE).

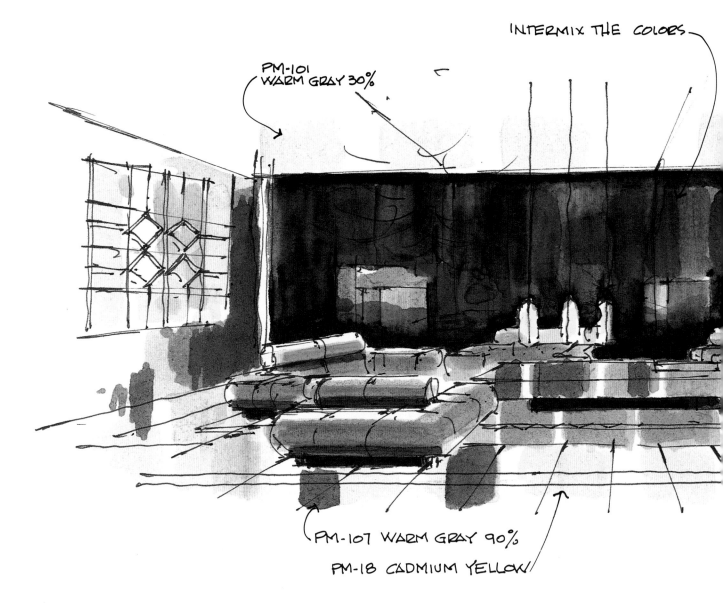

INTERMIX THE COLORS

PM-101
WARM GRAY 30%

PM-107 WARM GRAY 90%

PM-18 CADMIUM YELLOW

PM-18 CADMIUM YELLOW

PM-73 FLAGSTONE

PM-37 AQUAMARINE

APPLY THE FINAL TOUCHES.

TIME : 1 HOUR

PM-26
WILLOW GREEN

PM-32 REDWOOD

PM-34 OLIVE GREEN

WHITE MARKER

VERTICAL STROKES OF WHITE MARKER

PM-34 OLIVE GREEN

PM-82 REDWOOD

IVO DRPIC

LIVING ROOM
ARCHITECT: IVO D. DRPIC AND ASSOCIATES

## OPULENCE

THE LUXURIOUS EFFECT OF THIS
SPACE IS ACHIEVED PARTLY THROUGH
THE USE OF COLOR AND PARTLY
THROUGH THE FORMALISTIC COMPOSITION
OF THIS SKETCH.

BEGIN BY ROUGHLY INDICATING
THE SPACE AND BASIC FURNISHINGS.

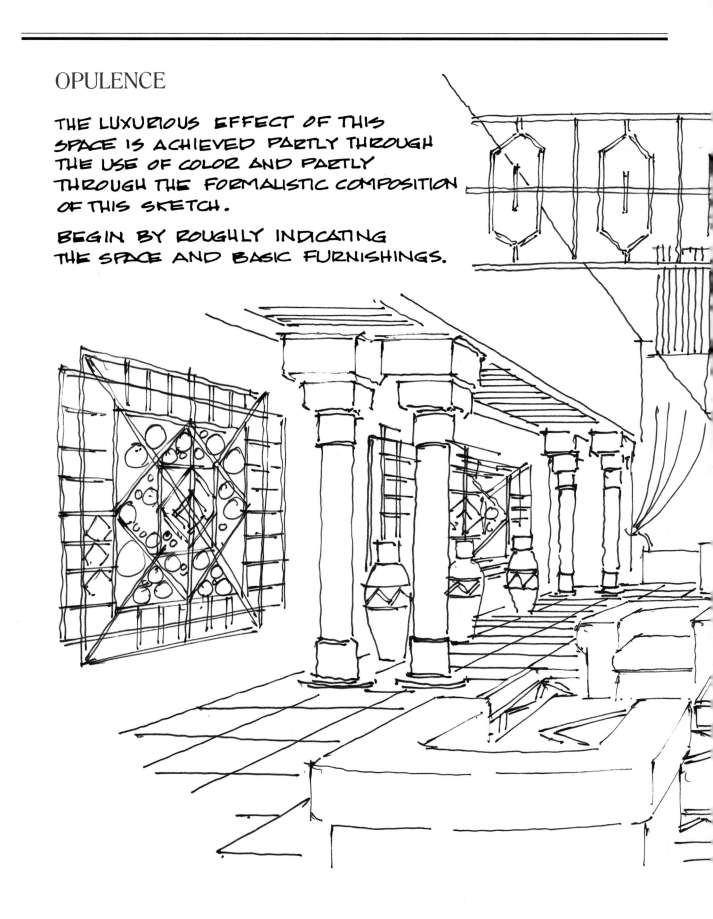

PM-IOI WARM GRAY 30%

APPLY COLORS AS SHOWN.

PM-51 GRAPE

PM-18 CADMIUM YELLOW

PM-67 SANGUINE

PM-91
LIGHT
GOTHIC OAK

PM-70 SAND

PM-52 CRANBERRY

PM-103 WARM GRAY 50%

PM-52 CRANBERRY

PANTONE 473-M

PM-18 CADMIUM YELLOW )

USE THE FINE AND BROAD TIPS OF A
SOFT COLOR MARKER ( HERE, PM-91
LIGHT GOTHIC OAK ) TO INTERMIX THE
PREVIOUSLY APPLIED COLORS.

PM-88 WALNUT

PM-98 BLACK

PM-67 SANGUINE

PM-105 WARM GRAY 70%

TOUCH UP WITH
WHITE MARKER

THE FINISHED SKETCH IS RICH
AND RESTRAINED.

LOBBY
ARCHITECT:
IVO D. DRPIC AND
ASSOCIATES

PM-2
CHINESE
RED

TOUCH UP WITH A SHARPIE PEN.

TOUCH UP WITH A
SHARPIE PEN

PM-51 GRAPE

PM-88
WALNUT

PM-41
FATHOM BLUE

IVO DRPIC

# COMFORT

THE RELAXED SENSE OF INFORMALITY THAT SUGGESTS COMFORT
IN THIS SUBURBAN RESIDENTIAL LIVING ROOM COMES FROM
THE USE OF TWO-POINT PERSPECTIVE, A RELATIVELY CLOSE-IN
VIEWPOINT, AND THE WAY COLOR HAS BEEN USED.

SKETCH THE SPACE FIRST WITHOUT COLOR.

APPLY THE SOFT-TONED COLORS FIRST,
BUILDING THEM UP GRADUALLY TO
ACHIEVE THE LOOK YOU WANT.

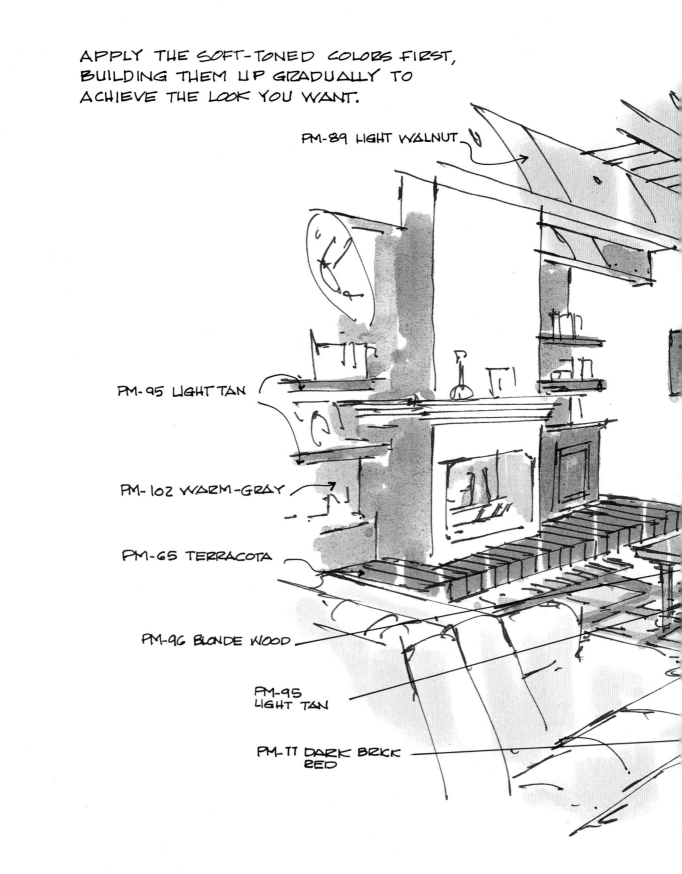

PM-89 LIGHT WALNUT

PM-95 LIGHT TAN

PM-102 WARM-GRAY

PM-65 TERRACOTA

PM-96 BLONDE WOOD

PM-95
LIGHT TAN

PM-77 DARK BRICK
RED

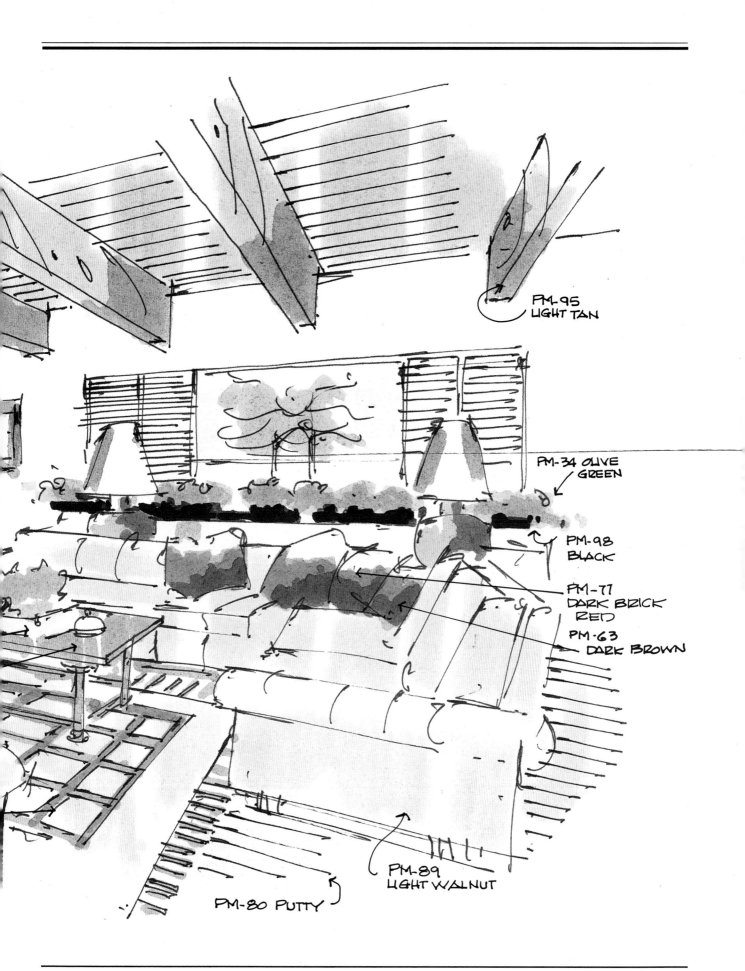

PM-95
LIGHT TAN

PM-34 OLIVE
GREEN

PM-98
BLACK

PM-77
DARK BRICK
RED

PM-63
DARK BROWN

PM-89
LIGHT WALNUT

PM-80 PUTTY

ADD THE DEEPER TONES.

PM-95 LIGHT TAN

PM-69 YELLOW OCHRE

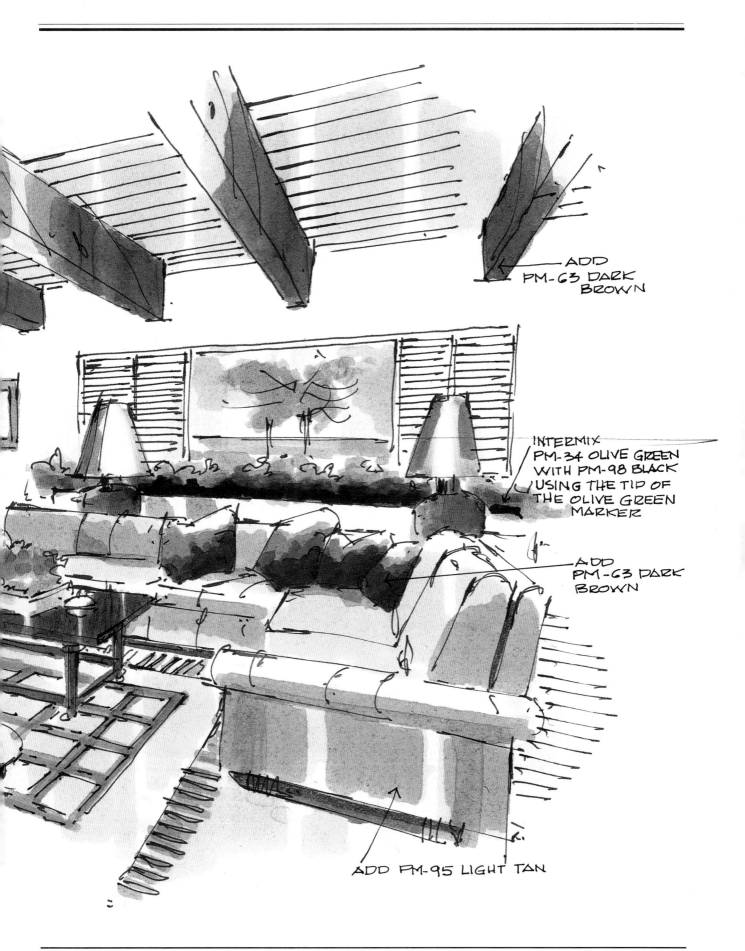

ADD
PM-63 DARK
BROWN

INTERMIX
PM-34 OLIVE GREEN
WITH PM-98 BLACK
USING THE TIP OF
THE OLIVE GREEN
MARKER

ADD
PM-63 DARK
BROWN

ADD PM-95 LIGHT TAN

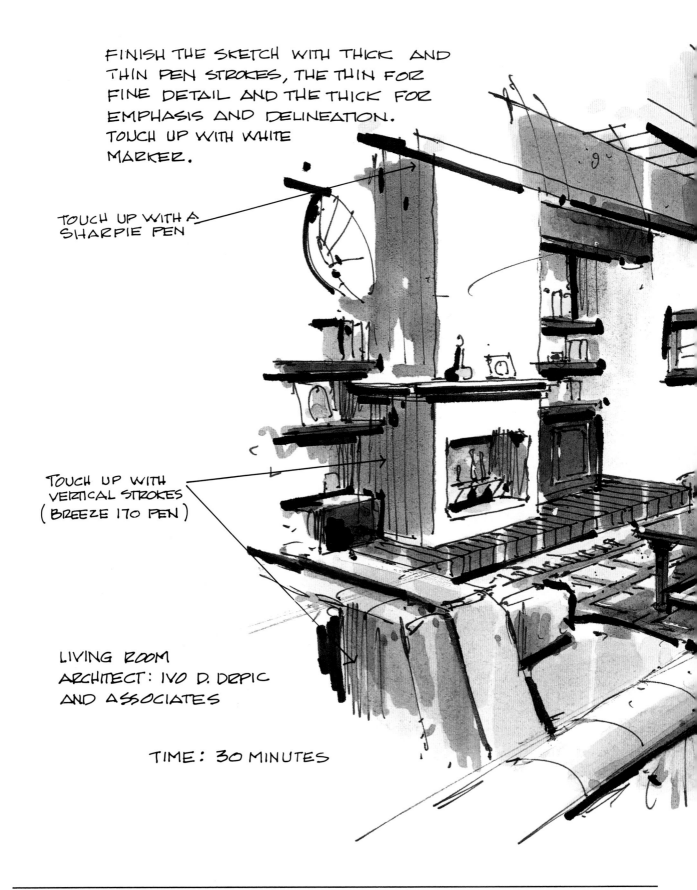

FINISH THE SKETCH WITH THICK AND THIN PEN STROKES, THE THIN FOR FINE DETAIL AND THE THICK FOR EMPHASIS AND DELINEATION. TOUCH UP WITH WHITE MARKER.

TOUCH UP WITH A SHARPIE PEN

TOUCH UP WITH VERTICAL STROKES (BREEZE 170 PEN)

LIVING ROOM
ARCHITECT: IVO D. DRPIC AND ASSOCIATES

TIME: 30 MINUTES

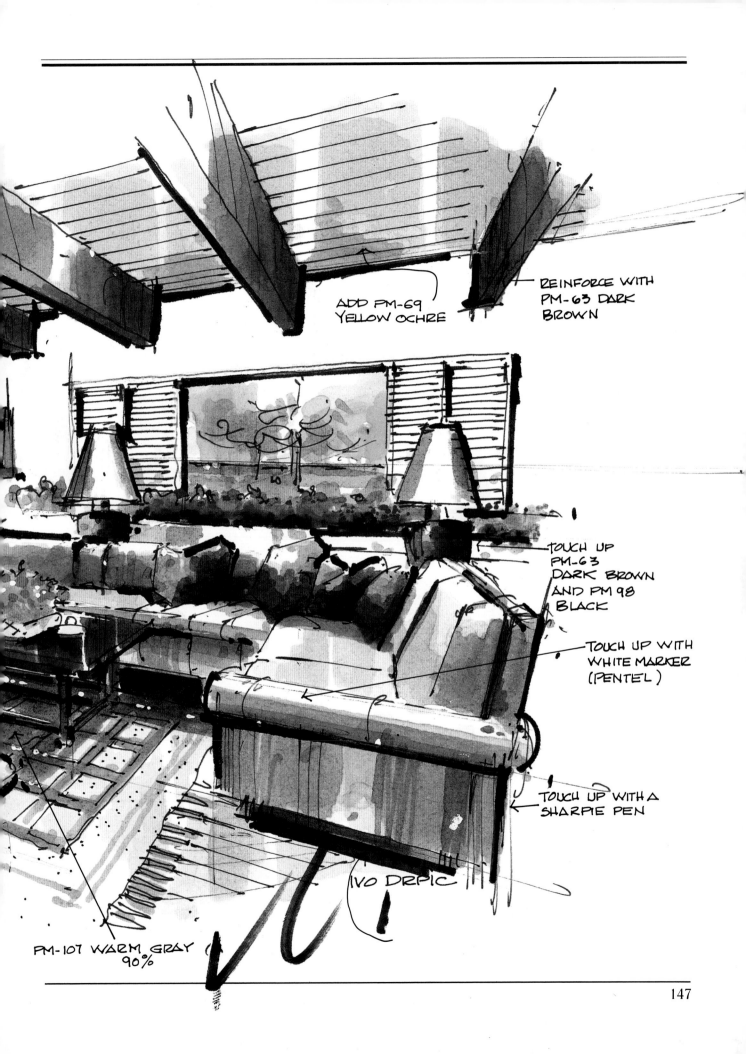

ADD PM-69
YELLOW OCHRE

REINFORCE WITH
PM-63 DARK
BROWN

TOUCH UP
PM-63
DARK BROWN
AND PM 98
BLACK

TOUCH UP WITH
WHITE MARKER
(PENTEL)

TOUCH UP WITH A
SHARPIE PEN

IVO DRPIC

PM-107 WARM GRAY
90%

# The Presentation

## SKETCHES FROM FOUR PORTFOLIOS

The designer's portfolio is a communicator of conceptual and visual information to other design professionals as well as to clients. It is also a powerful selling tool. This section offers a representative portfolio sampling from four different kinds of interiors projects: offices and hotels, residences, health care facilities, and malls.

**Presentation Sketch for BNR Inc.,
Research Park Triangle, North Carolina**
Architect: CRSS, Inc., Houston, Texas

# OFFICE INTERIORS

Pages 150 through 161 illustrate sketches from three
different projects. They range from two preliminary
studies—in the opened gatefold and on these two
pages—to a presentation-quality sketch and a rough
concept sketch flanking the gatefold. Only one
of them took more than three hours from start to finish.

**Presentation Sketch of Offices for BNR Inc.,
Research Triangle Park, North Carolina**

Architects, Engineers, Interior Architects: CRSS, Inc., Houston, Texas
Medium: Nylon tip pen and colored markers on sketch paper
Size: 24 inches by 28 inches
Time: 3 hours

**Preliminary Study of a Hotel Atrium, Houston, Texas**
Architect: Ivo D. Drpic and Associates, Houston, Texas
Medium: Nylon tip pen and colored markers on sketch paper
Size: 20 inches by 40 inches
Time: 8 hours

IVO DRPIC/87

**Preliminary Study of Offices for Houtronics, Houston, Texas**
Architect: Ivo D. Drpic and Associates
Medium: Nylon tip pen and colored markers on sketch paper
Size: 14 inches by 18 inches
Time: 3 hours

**Concept Sketch for Hudson Engineering Corporation, Houston, Texas**
Project Architects: Jack M. Reber and Ivo D. Drpic
Medium: Nylon tip pen and colored markers on sketch paper
Size: 36 inches by 7 inches
Time: 2 hours

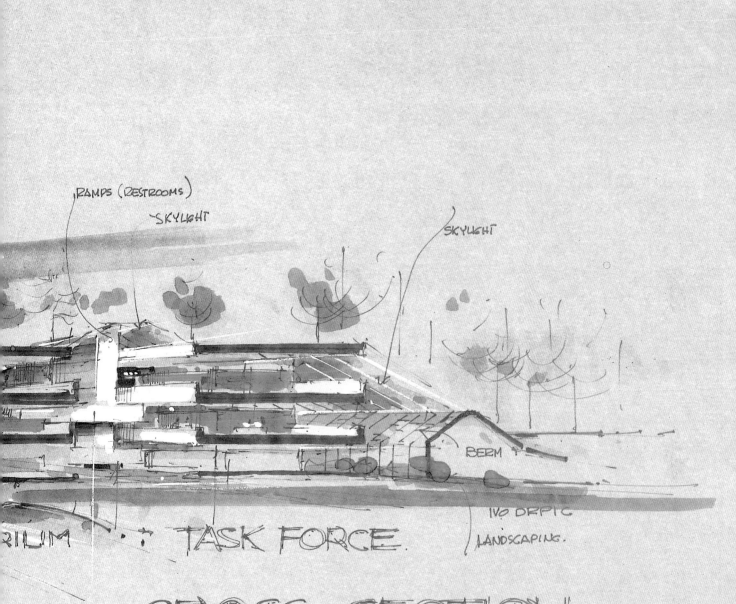

RAMPS (RESTROOMS)

SKYLIGHT

SKYLIGHT

BERM

RIUM · · TASK FORCE.

IVO DRPIC

LANDSCAPING.

CROSS SECTION.
PRELIMINARY CONCEPT

# RESIDENTIAL INTERIORS

Three preliminary studies for use in design development show how much effect can be achieved in very little time. The sketches on these two pages were executed in less than twenty minutes each. The living room on pages 162 and 163 required only about an hour and a half.

**Preliminary Study of a Living Room**
Architect: Ivo D. Drpic and Associates, Houston, Texas
Medium: Nylon tip pen and colored markers on sketch paper
Size: 8 inches by 10 inches
Time: 20 minutes

IVO DRPIC

**Preliminary Study of a Living Room**
Architect: Ivo D. Drpic and Associates, Houston, Texas
Medium: Nylon tip pen and colored markers on sketch paper
Size: 8 inches by 10 inches
Time: 20 minutes

163

**Preliminary Study for a Living Room**
Architect: Ivo D. Drpic and Associates, Houston, Texas
Medium: Nylon tip pen and colored markers on sketch paper
Size: 18 inches by 24 inches
Time: 1½ hours

# HEALTH CARE FACILITY INTERIORS

These sketches are actually of presentation-rendering quality
and are sufficiently detailed and finished to be publishable.
Yet using the methods presented in this book, neither
required more than four-and-a-half hours to complete.

**Presentation Sketch for a Dental Clinic
in Baumholder, West Germany**
Architect: The Falick/Klein Partnership, Inc.; Steffen + Peter
Project Architect: Jerry Turner
Interior Designer: Wendy Buonodono
Medium: Nylon tip pen and colored markers on sketch paper
Size: 16 inches by 24 inches
Time: 4 hours

IVO DRPIC 9/87

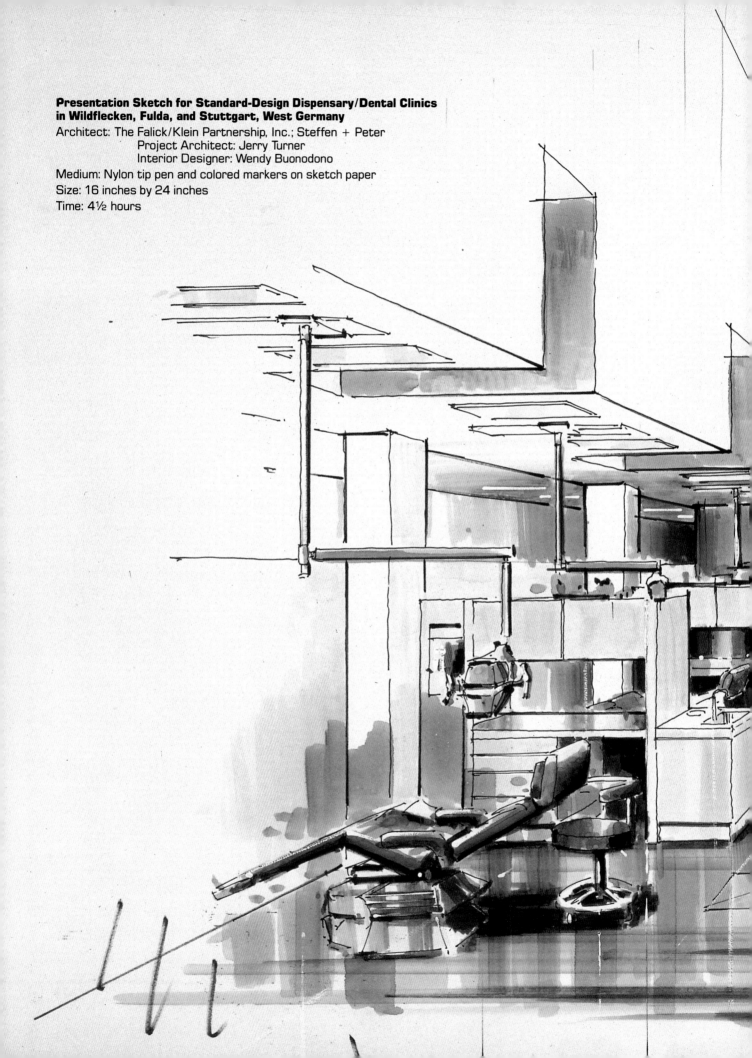

**Presentation Sketch for Standard-Design Dispensary/Dental Clinics
in Wildflecken, Fulda, and Stuttgart, West Germany**
Architect: The Falick/Klein Partnership, Inc.; Steffen + Peter
                    Project Architect: Jerry Turner
                    Interior Designer: Wendy Buonodono
Medium: Nylon tip pen and colored markers on sketch paper
Size: 16 inches by 24 inches
Time: 4½ hours

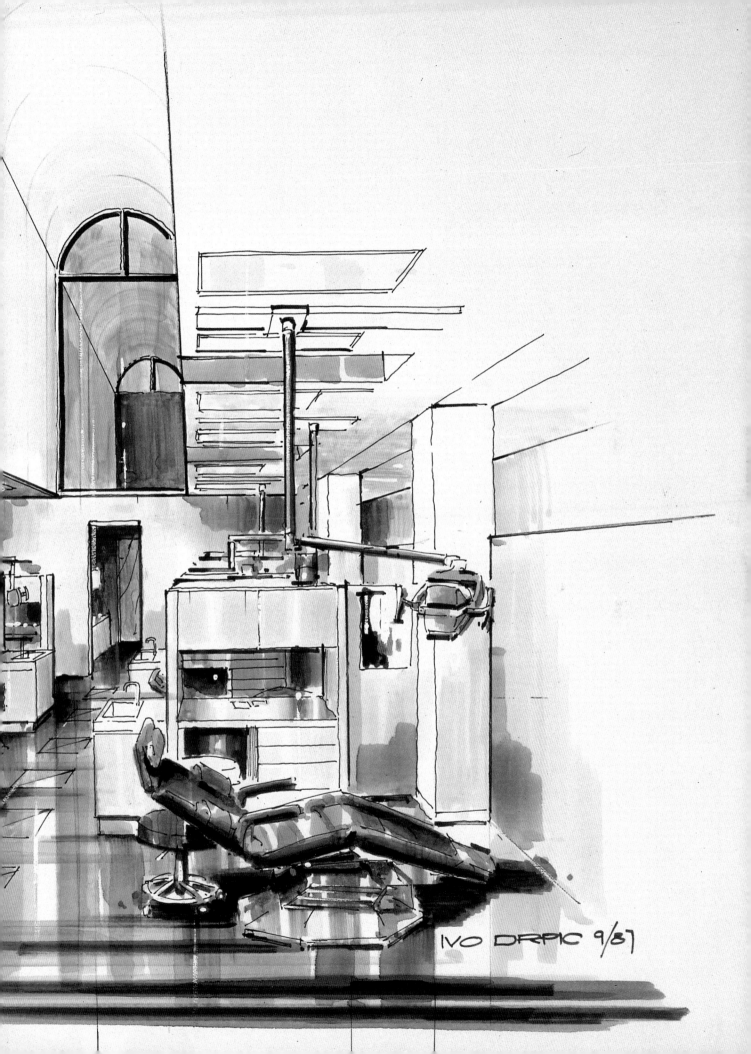

IVO DRPIC 9/87

# MALLS

These sketches convey the scale and
feeling of two different malls with
and economy of line, color, and time.

170

**Preliminary Concept Sketch for a Shopping Center in Houston, Texas**
Architect: Ivo D. Drpic and Associates
Medium: Nylon tip pen and colored markers on sketch paper
Size: 36 inches by 17 inches
Time: 2 hours

**Preliminary Study for Sugarland Mall, Sugarland, Texas**
Architect: Ivo D. Drpic and Associates, Houston, Texas
Medium: Nylon tip pen and colored markers on sketch paper
Size: 14 inches by 14 inches
Time: 1 hour

CAPEZIO'S

LIPTONS

NO DRPIC /89

**Concept Sketch for a Hotel Atrium in Miami, Florida**
Architect: Ivo D. Drpic and Associates
Medium: Nylon tip pen and colored markers on sketch paper
Size: 30 inches by 30 inches
Time: 10 hours

# Index